DIMLY LIT MEALS FOR ONE

TOM KENNEDY

HEARTBREAKING TALES OF SAD FOOD
AND EVEN SADDER LIVES

JOHN BLAKE

Published by John Blake Publishing Ltd,
3 Bramber Court, 2 Bramber Road,
London W14 9PB, England

www.johnblakebooks.com

www.facebook.com/johnblakebooks 🛐
twitter.com/jblakebooks 🅴

This edition published in 2015

ISBN: 978 1 78418 689 0

British Library Cataloguing-in-Publication Data:

A catalogue record for this book is available from the British Library.

Design by www.envydesign.co.uk

Printed and bound by Zrinski D.D, Croatia.

1 3 5 7 9 10 8 6 4 2

Papers used by John Blake Publishing are natural, recyclable products made from wood grown in sustainable
forests. The manufacturing processes conform to the environmental regulations of the country of origin.

Every attempt has been made to contact the relevant copyright-holders, but some were unobtainable. We would
be grateful if the appropriate people could contact us.

INTRODUCTION

Imagine the scene: it's a couple of weeks after Christmas and you're standing in a medium-sized WHSmiths. Burning its way through the pocket of your corduroy trousers is a £10 book token from your favourite aunt.

In one hand you clasp the delightful Delia Smith's perennial classic, *One is Fun!* In the other, you hold internet-nobody Tom Kennedy's grim tome, *Dimly Lit Meals for One.*

You only have one limited-value book token to spend – which one do you pick?

Be careful, the decision will have lasting consequences.

You see this isn't like the *Choose Your Own Adventure* books of yesteryear, where you could read ahead and cheat yourself out of the character-building experience of true failure.

No.

One book embodies the spirit of optimism, perseverance and self-assured independence.

It will teach you that mealtimes needn't be lonely, that you don't have to live off a diet of tinned hotdogs and stolen packets of ketchup, surrounded by your own filth and crying over John Lewis adverts.

The other is a cynical cash-in based on a blog that was briefly popular in early 2014, written by a bitter failure of a human consumed by self-loathing and driven to write bleak prose inspired by unattractive plates of food.

It will teach you nothing save the author's myriad prejudices and staggering insecurities.

You may feel better about yourself, but only through vicariously experiencing the far worse lives of entirely fictitious others.

Of course, you might just find something within that is a little too close to your own solitary existence for comfort.

So, which one do you pick?

I've got to assume by now that you felt too self-conscious standing next to the remaindered books section reading through a book of bad food photography and rambling stories.

Social awkwardness compelled you to make a rash decision and purchase *Dimly Lit Meals for One*; now you're sitting alone at home experiencing buyer's remorse while somewhere, perhaps not so very far away, my sales figures finally break into double digits.

Thanks for that.

While you're here, do you want to hang out some time?

Maybe we could get a pizza and a couple of beers, or go see a local band?

It doesn't even matter if they're crap. I'd just like to get out of the flat for a bit, if I'm honest.

Anything really, I'm happy to do whatever.

I haven't even begun to think about dinner.

I don't think I can face cooking tonight.

Tom Kennedy, 2015

4

6

It's fairly straightforward recreating the feeling that you're confined in a drab, urine-sodden, government institution, circa 1979.

All you need is a big blue tray, mildly racist comedy on the TV, and the pervasive threat of sexual harassment from one of the wildly popular 'creepy uncle' models of presenter so prevalent during British light-entertainment's darkest decade.

Unlike their terrified leisure-suit-clad counterparts in Britain's darkest decade, today's home cook not only lives free from a constant fear of abuse and loud unexpected noises, but is also able to purchase an approximation of the cuisine of different cultures in frozen form. They can even have it delivered straight to the door – all while sitting on fire-retardant sofas bathed in the warm glow of wide-screen televisions, in silent appreciation of one of the rapidly diminishing pool of television personalities not yet conclusively proven to be molesters.

For those, however, who still feel a painful longing for the era that gave the world Texan bars, space hoppers and dirty protests there exist whole industries geared towards making them feel more comfortable on this confusing, now less-prejudiced, planet.

One could, if one wished, spend all one's disposable income on obtaining important cultural artifacts through eBay, such as the complete set of Wombles annuals (in mint to mildly soiled condition), exciting solo LPs from Steve Howe of Yes, and the James Callaghan Action Man every child of the seventies dreamed of receiving for Christmas.

It's now possible to wholly insulate yourself from the feeling that you're trapped in a world you never made. To sit with your big blue prison tray in front of a never-ending loop of the *On the Buses* films, Liverpool winning the 1977 European Cup final, and grainy footage of Noel Edmonds standing in front of a smouldering tower of uncollected rubbish, maniacally urging a reluctant daredevil to leap over it in their Kawasaki Z900.

The French used to refer to the British as 'les rosbifs' because we were once upon a time – in addition to our innate love of fair play and good manners – renowned for a collective fondness for sitting around in Harvesters eating overcooked cow flesh, invariably washed down with a foaming pint of warm beer.

Globalisation and corporate homogeneity put an end to all that and now Britons are far more likely to spend their evenings in with a microwaved burger and a can of ice-cold pissy Australian lager, abusing a stranger on Twitter and voting UKIP for a laugh.

There's a reason the French updated their Breton-striped slang dictionaries and re-branded us 'les fuckoffs': we've become a staggeringly rude shitheap of badly behaved cunts who've forgotten how to 'ros' their 'bifs'.

I'm not necessarily writing a lament for days gone by – to my palate warm beer tastes a lot

like stomach lining, and experience has taught me that very polite people are usually up to their necks in petty workplace larceny or leading the sort of double life where they put house cats in wheelie bins and occasionally vandalise the nearby Princess Diana memorial under the cover of darkness.

You probably know the sort well: the kindly Mary Berry-type, seemingly all sweetness and light but betrayed by a certain flintiness in the eyes, who is consistently disgusted by the antics of your Jonathan Rosses and your Russell Brands, yet periodically finds themselves embroiled in a vicious poison-pen-letter campaign against a fellow member of the WI who had the temerity to suggest their Bundt cakes were 'a bit dry for their liking'.

The saddest meals aren't always the unhealthiest ones.

For every lonely tray of burnt turkey dinosaurs and potato faces eaten in front of *Top Gear* by a solitary alcoholic in their forties, there's an equally miserable bowl of microwaved green beans and spinach noodles topped with an egg being prepared by someone who's looking to diet and jog their way out of the black cloud of despair that has engulfed them. Sometimes the worst thing in the world isn't the food that makes you hate yourself after you eat, but the food you're unable to eat without hating humanity itself.

The all-powerful microwave lobby contends that, contrary to what the Soviets believed when they banned them in the late seventies, rather than turning your carrots into self-aware radioactive abominations, using a microwave can actually help to preserve nutrients.

So if you believe large corporations and the doctors they employ (and why wouldn't you?), microwaving your veg might be beneficial to your health. But to that I say, 'At what cost to your soul?'

Like many literature graduates I couldn't actually tell you *how* a microwave works, although I have a vague awareness that it involves depleted uranium and that because it cooks food outwards from the core you need to turn your meals inside out before zapping them, similar to the way you'd wash a T-shirt with a hard-to-iron design on its front.

The puddle of rust-coloured vegetable juice gathering at the bottom of your microwaveable dish that you pour out along with your rubbery veg, instantly regretting being too lazy to drain it off as it runs into your mashed potatoes, creating a small heap of slurry that will sit reproachfully on your plate as if asking you why you couldn't have just had frozen peas.

The unrelenting corporatisation of British university life has meant that the fondly remembered cliché of the right-on scholarly slacker unwilling to rise before midday, determinedly spending their student grant on subsidised beer to be enjoyed in the union bar, fervently discussing Sartre and experimenting with asymmetrical haircuts is sadly no more.

Unfortunately, for those of us whose expectations and understanding of what student culture might consist of was indelibly shaped by watching *The Young Ones*, our fictional antiheroes of yesteryear have been replaced by a generation of single-minded careerist students encouraged to think of themselves as customers and treat higher education as a stepping stone towards landing a job involving spreadsheets or something that earns that coveted 'ever so slightly above average' pay grade.

This is because, as you're surely aware, a human being's worth is directly proportionate to how much money they earn. Students are blank canvases with the potential to make lots of money and become great people, like a YouTube blogger or a Jeremy Clarkson.

This all means that today's students are more into 'getting their money's worth', 'avoiding debt', and 'going to lectures', which leaves them fewer opportunities to forget they've got an exam the next day and freak out on psilocybin mushroom.

There are, however, a few exceptions: students who are already financially secure or simply tragically impulsive may still elect to supplement their degree in anthropology with an elective in ketamine studies and an introduction to malnutrition.

This lifestyle choice is nicely illustrated in the corresponding photograph: observe the massive multipack of crisps and half-eaten value range microwaveable meal alongside a highly suspect jar, which may or may not contain urine.

Putting aside the fact that it almost certainly contains the stale piss of a young man too scared and too high to have ventured out of his bedroom to go and make use of the communal facilities, this is a wonderful snapshot of the eating habits of a member of this increasingly endangered breed of tertiary education tosspot.

13

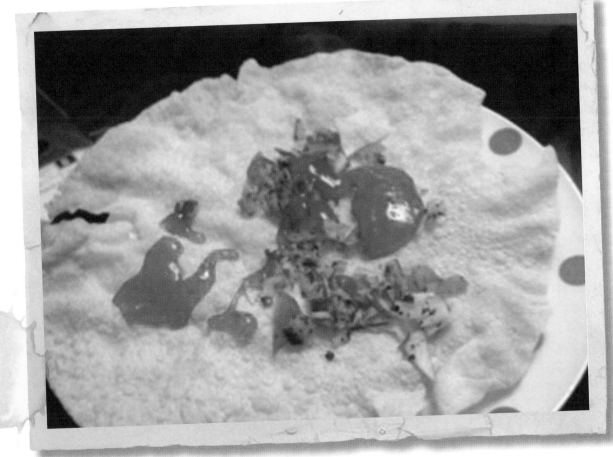

You blew the whole month's food budget on a takeaway Indian meal for two that you ate alone, and now you're paying the price.

Three days later the poppadoms have long lost their crunch and now yield unpleasantly to your cautious and exploratory nibbling. Yet you are so hungry that you pile on the last desperate scrapings of the complementary chutney pots, fairly confident that while rancid, it won't actually kill you.

Whatever compelled you to take to the skies like Icarus and circle so perilously around the blazing hot sun of financial insolvency?

You knew you couldn't afford another Friday night in gorging yourself on curry someone else reheated for you, but the pervasive advertisements of the online fast-food middlemen were so persuasive that you once again allowed yourself to become overdrawn all for the momentary convenience of having a friendly stranger appear at the door and hand over a bag of rapidly cooling dhansak.

'Why cook?' the cynical cavorting comedy chefs seductively whispered to you as you sat half-naked, bathed in the television's warm glow.

'Cooking is for rubes and the suckers who don't know how to manage their time; you could spend all evening slaving over a hot stove and have nothing to show for it save a saucepan covered in burnt-on rice.

'You're living in the twenty-first century, not Stalin's Russia.

'You're a junior-level administrator with the world by the balls.

'You can afford to have the good people of Curry Emporium do the hard work!

'Now, put your feet up and enjoy the mild state-sanctioned banter of two offensively anodyne presenters on the BBC's flagship *One Show* quizzing Katie Hopkins on her opinions about reintroducing the death penalty for cyclists, the overweight and people who say "pacifically" instead of "specifically".'

For the shit home cook a bottle of ketchup is much more than a mere condiment.

It can be the only means of disguising that ever-so-slightly spoiled food you're too cheap to throw out.

The bloody red sauce adds a splash of colour to an otherwise drab plate of chips and Turkey Dinosaurs. Turkey Dinosaurs, the purchase of which caused the young cashier at Morrisons eyebrows to rise all the way up her forehead like a pair of caterpillars pulled by a hook.

As if there was somehow something sinister about a balding man in NHS spectacles with a basket full of children's food, a large jar of petroleum jelly and several rolls of duct tape doing his shop at half past eleven on a Wednesday night.

A well-stocked sauce cupboard reminds me of the longest winter of my life spent temping in a Human Resources department that was awful, even by the low standards of HR.

I remember receiving an insanely optimistic job application for *every single job* going on the company website, the opening sentence of which boasted of the applicant's 'can-do attitude' and that 'with the help of Google search, I can work on any technology'.

Imagine that. *Any technology*.

With my well-stocked sauce cupboard I can eat *any* food.

As long as I have some strong flavours to mask the taste of burning and despair, preferably involving a healthy dose of vinegar or a spicy chilli, I can pretty much stomach whatever cruel fate has sought fit to squat down and dump out all over my plate.

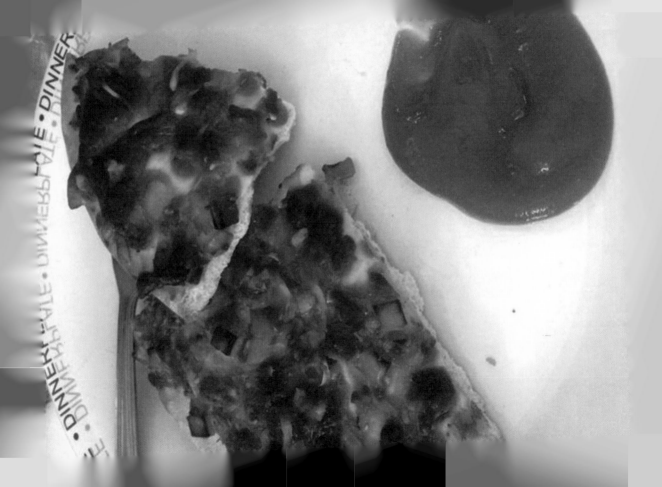

Loneliness can be an overwhelming emotion.

We lead increasingly isolated lives viewing everything through the distorted prism of manipulated newsfeeds and stage-managed 'reality' shows, all ultra hi-def, on ultra-flat screens.

The sense of dislocation one can feel from the outside world is only amplified by a tide of images from social media and lifestyle programming depicting other people's impossibly perfect, unbearably smug lives. Lives in which the most profound obstacle a human being can overcome is finding the right interior decorator to help realise their vision of renovating a medieval friary in a manner that reflects a twin love of both hardcore normcore and Scandinavian boxset neo-minimalism.

For someone whose only companion is the lingering smell of death coming from behind the fridge, the life these *other* people lead can appear as a series of highly expensive fetishised acquisitions, plucked straight from the lifestyle pages of an upmarket broadsheet.

These people have never felt the pain of seeing their bucket of greying sludge fall into a shitty sink and having nothing left for lunch.

They've never trimmed the mouldy edges off a slice of supermarket own-brand white and hoped the toaster will sufficiently kill off any lingering bacteria so they don't wind up getting sick and caught short running for the bus.

No, these people, these people are not like you and I.

We never had successful careers in the city that we then gave up to enjoy a rural idyll in Brontë country.

We don't have frosty ash-blonde partners called Tabitha, who gave up modelling to wear Alice bands and start a free school, supporting us wholeheartedly in our ambitions to live out the rest of our lives as artisan bread-makers, or hipster blacksmiths, or boutique taxidermists.

We are the rancid cottage cheese, spiralling down the drain, clogging up the pipes, stinking out the flat.

Ian, yet again you've been spotted hanging around Gavin's desk, mucking about with your phone, taking pictures of each other's lunch when you should have been over at reception covering Becky's break.

You know full well she's hypoglycaemic; if Martin hadn't brought her over a flapjack I dread to think what might have happened.

Please, Ian, you should know by now that this carefully constructed persona revolving exclusively around a tedious nostalgia for a barely remembered eighties childhood is getting on everybody's nerves.

I don't want to be loudly reminded about *Roland Rat* every time Roland Rodriguez from the Madrid office calls up

To be perfectly frank with you, Ian, I don't give a fuck about the Marathon vs Snickers debate. It's been twenty-five years; you need to get over it.

For Pete's sake, Ian, you're a grown man!

We covered this in your last appraisal.

You need to stop wearing your *Danger Mouse* tie into the operations meeting every Friday. You might not be dealing directly with clients since you were transferred into the basement but that doesn't mean we've given up trying to enforce the dress code.

It's not even a proper tie, Ian. It's a clip-on.

At least when Gavin in accounts brings his *Simpsons* one in on his birthday you can tell it's 100 per cent silk.

First thing to go, though, is that bloody mug.

You're not a robot in disguise, Ian.

You're a twat.

21

When single people get sick they have no one to make miserable with their suffering and, unless they're willing to move back in with their parents into an old childhood bedroom that now houses an assortment of vintage jukeboxes, they are forced to shoulder the burden of their illness alone.

There is an unspoken agreement among most couples that when it comes time for one of them to fill up with snot, there is some reciprocity of sympathy, which means that when their time comes they'll have a lackey on hand to fetch enough painkillers and Lucozade to get them through what is usually a bad hangover and not weapons-grade Ebola.

Those who dine alone do not have such a luxury.

They know that when they're struck down by the lurgy there's a very real chance they could die alone and not be discovered until their colleagues realise the unusual smell in the office has gone and begin to put two and two together.

You can't afford to wallow in self-pity. You need to get strong and fend off the sickness that has prompted your body to assume the foetal position under a heavy feather duvet (washed, since you bought it, a grand total of zero times).

It's time for you roll out of bed and find the eye of the tiger.

You don't have a walk-in freezer with big slabs of meat to beat, so you do the next best thing and try to eat yourself back from the brink of death.

You break out the multivitamins, hide the booze, fags and chocolate, and try in your own pathetic way to replicate the diet of someone who hasn't effectively given up on life.

The result is like a child's drawing of what a healthy person might eat: a big bowl of amorphous green sludge, a frantic blend of spinach and broccoli, two and a half pints of Linda Blair's sick.

Alone in her darkened corner of the office again, everyone else having sneaked off to Nando's to gossip about her, Sarah stares intently at the mashed-up fish and cucumber that she's spread all over the sliced brown bread.

Sometimes she likes to chase down her open-faced fish sandwiches with a couple of vitamins and a selective serotonin reuptake inhibitor.

At the moment it's a case of taking things one day at a time.

It doesn't help, though, that the thought of the factory-farmed salmon now smeared all over her toast had lived a life of agony, covered in great big parasitic worms, confined to a tiny fish prison.

It makes her dwell on the casual cruelty meted out by mankind towards every other living creature in existence either in the name of industrial agriculture or through simple old-fashioned sadistic malevolence.

Mealtimes like this were brutal.

Sarah feels like hurling her sandwich against the Tom Hiddleston calendar decorating her cubicle wall and screaming 'WHY ME, GOD, WHY ME?' for all the office to hear.

Of course, they wouldn't hear her.

They were out eating Piri Piri chicken and talking about the weird woman who couldn't make small talk by the photocopier.

Sadly, Sarah realises, life doesn't magically right itself after you leave school and join the world of work. You won't suddenly be liked because you get on with things quietly and don't make a fuss.

Life remains a popularity contest, a game with no clear rulebook, where people smile to your face and then circulate companywide emails about 'unpleasant food odours' coming from people's desks.

The tall man in the brand new Burton suit reclines, louche and assured, completely at ease on your dead mum's faux Italian leather sofa, munching on pitta and drinking warm beer.

The remote, self-doubting part of you is unable to believe you are really enjoying mealtime banter with a man who's sold a house to Jeremy Clarkson's cousin.

He pulls a hilarious face as he loudly passes wind into your mum's favourite decorative cushion.

You giggle like a schoolboy.

It feels somehow shameful that you can only offer the runner-up 2012 Estate Agent of the Year (Rhyl and Prestatyn area) a pitta and a stolen pint glass not quite filled by the warm can of Red Stripe you pour into it.

Ever since Mother passed on, you've been unaccustomed to company, especially the sort that turns up for a tour of his client's house in a top-of-the-line Fiat 500.

'Bottom line, I'm going to sell the shit out of this house. Get rid of all the chintz, paint everything nice and neutral like. Use some of this Lynx Africa to get rid of the old lady smell and we'll be laughing.

'Another thing… try baking some bread when you've got people over having a look. They go mad for that. Make sure you get all these tinnies out of the front room, cut back on the cheese you're eating in here, air it out good and proper. It'll be absolutely lovely.'

For the first time since Mother rode the stairlift to heaven you feel a deep, almost spiritual connection with another human being.

Basking in this guy's presence is like being invited to the popular lads' party at school.

Only this time you've not been asked along so they can tie you up, superglue their pubes onto your face to fashion a crude beard, and then spend the rest of the year calling you Noel Edmonds.

Drinking out of jam jars.

It's all meant to evoke the spirit of Prohibition, which we didn't have in England, and seems to be popular with the sort of people who are heavily into burlesque but also like to listen to rockabilly and have recently just gotten into roller derby.

People in their late twenties, yearning to have been born several decades earlier but also incapable of living without the internet. People who are deeply confused about exactly which decade it is that they're pretending to live in at any one time.

The Prohibition period was clearly a great bunch of laughs.

The bizarre moral prescriptions of a fanatical minority led to a black market in moonshine so brain-meltingly strong that it could turn a Professor Brian Cox into a Brian Conley.

Everyone wore smart hats.

Gangsters had nifty nicknames like 'Dutch' or 'Machine Gun' or 'Murderous Ian'.

The jars were used out of necessity; they were containers doubling as drinking vessels that could yield a lot more bootleg booze than your standard martini glass.

Why did they become popular again?

Does it really matter?

Maybe some enterprising lad with a handlebar moustache found a load of them in his dead gran's attic and was inspired to start a pop-up saloon.

Next year it'll be something else.

Syringes, probably.

A cheeky little nod to Pete Doherty, just in time for a Libertines revival.

It's a cold January morning and Portia Totes-Bants sits cross-legged on the floor of a bedsit in Peckham.

The recent graduate of Central Saint Martins and self-proclaimed 'ramen terrorist' has emerged as the de facto chronicler of fashionable London noodle bar Brennschluss.

Portia spent much of 2014 deliberately baiting Charles Campion of the *London Evening Standard* with her confrontational concept menu, '1,000 Limp Noodles & Other Wok Suckers', and witnessed the capital's infatuation with what many people are calling 'Chinese Spaghetti' reach saturation point.

Portia sits cross-legged on the floor of her extraordinarily small bathroom, giving herself a homemade haircut in front of the mirror.

Apologising for the lack of tea, she explains that 'some fascists from the Met came here last Wednesday and took away my kettle'.

Portia brushes the remnants of a hastily trimmed bastard fringe out of her eyes and casually nibbles on an uncooked brick of ramen.

'It's interesting because it looks shit, yeah?

'And it doesn't really taste good either; it's like a statement about the commodification of food.

'I mean, here's a bowl of soggy noodles and some old microwaved carrot and I'm charging you, like, over twenty pounds for it.

'I'm pretty much the only chef in London who's honest about how much they hate food and the people who eat it.'

Early on in life, many of us learn to substitute the difficult human currencies of love and affection for the simpler, less-demanding embrace of refined sugar.

Sweet things are always there for us: they are constant, unchanging and utterly reliable.

They won't sleep with your best friend, have a midlife crisis, wear overly tight jeans, or start spending their days online, secretly making insensate, possibly racist, comments on *Guardian* articles.

Unlike a cat, desserts won't constantly fail to shit in the litterbox correctly and then break your heart by getting sick and dying.

Desserts will always be happy to see you and even if they rot your teeth and almost certainly lead to you needing a foot amputated somewhere down the line, they're still far less dangerous a lover than an average adult male.

So here you are, standing atop your very own baked Beachy Head, looking out over a sea of custard stretching out towards infinity, imagining the warm creamy waves enveloping your body like the cloying embrace of an over-perfumed elderly aunt.

The small piece of apple pie is barely visible under the thick canary-yellow tide. A token portion there to give licence to the gallons and gallons of custard you've been fantasising about cooking up and gorging yourself on ever since the moment you arrived at your draughty workplace and saw sweet sad-eyed Andrew from Finance holding hands with that awful cow Linda.

It felt like all the air was escaping from your lungs; you were overcome by an overwhelming desire to replace all that poisoned blood flowing through your hardened veins with sweet, loyal crème Anglaise.

It's not easy holding down a steady job and still finding the time to cram in a minimum of five pints during your lunch break.

The high-calorie content in beer enables your belly to snugly fit into your rumpled Salvation Army suit trousers, but sadly there's a startling lack of affordable dining options in the local boozer to top it up with non-alcoholic nourishment.

Over the years, many a traditional British pub has subtly morphed from a dingy, smoky dive with two guest ales and a red-faced racist landlord into a crypto-foodie hangout run by a plump-cheeked toff with a burning need to serve highly obscure cuts of meat atop jagged plates fashioned from reclaimed driftwood.

You don't want to risk wasting beer money on a lamb burger that could well have been stuffed full of fennel, yet experience has taught you that staggering back into the office with nothing inside you to soak up the booze would be a very bad idea.

Questions are still being asked about the two and a half tons of aqua gravel purchased in error on the company credit card, still occupying three car parking spaces, unable to be returned.

Perusing the menu that's been handwritten in chalk on slate, you find nothing to whet your appetite.

Bloody expensive.

Far too many herbs.

Not sure which part of the animal that's from, if it's from an animal at all.

Sweat beads on your forehead.

The stink of indecision rises from you like a smoke signal.

At that moment the bartender takes pity on you, offering the emergency Peperami from under the bar.

You gratefully scarf it down like a hungry dog, along with a packet of cheese and onion crisps.

Now, on to pint number three.

It's difficult, but you have to accept that sometimes the frozen pizza you bought and lovingly raised in your freezer for so many months doesn't want to be a pizza.

Daddy's little pizza is all grown up now; it's choosing to live as a calzone and you need to be understanding and respectful of its wishes.

Spend some time educating yourself about calzones.

You'll soon find out they're basically just a pizza folded in half. You'll get some people saying there's more to them than that but they're wrong – it's quite clearly a folded pizza.

Putting flatbread semantics to one side, calzones deserve to be recognised as having their own distinct identity separate from their unfolded brethren.

Of course, it's primarily an identity that's based upon arguments about how you pronounce the name.

Do you say cal-ZONE as if you're in an episode of *Seinfeld*? Or do you do what a genuine Italian would do (other than wear sunglasses and hang around the Hard Rock Cafe) and call it a cal-ZONI?

It's quite evident that calzones simply don't inspire anywhere near the same all-encompassing devotion that the more famous flatbread inspires from its acned acolytes. A recent survey of American teenagers found an astonishing 46 per cent listed their sexual identity as 'pizza'.

Obviously, someone needs to raise awareness about calzones.

That person is you.

You would think that working in a restaurant came with a few perks.

Obviously, you have to work unsociable hours, and you'd be extremely lucky if you never chopped off the tip of the odd finger here and there, but surely you get to take the leftovers home and you never go hungry on the job, right?

No, sadly this is untrue.

Just as working in a library or a bookstore doesn't mean you get to spend all day looking up swear words in the dictionary, neither does working around filet mignon mean you get the best of beef worlds.

Unless, of course, like the millions and millions of other criminally-minded wage slaves across the globe, you're heavily involved in petty theft from work.

The honest kitchen worker has to make do with far less-appetising fare.

Like the poor sap who faced the end of a gruelling twelve-hour shift with this: a sad slice of American cheese in garish Homer Simpson yellow melted over a stale slice of ciabatta and covered in what appears to be a small child's handwriting practice.

Brutal.

Such exploitation, such callous indifference to the plight of the working man.

No wonder the restaurant staff all take turns pissing in the vichyssoise.

Even when taking into consideration such charmers as the sods behind the Salem Witch Trials or the feckless shits responsible for the decline of the Roman Empire, the Baby Boomers, as time will undoubtedly bear out, were the absolute worst generation in the whole of recorded history.

Unlike the generation before them who worked so hard to defeat Nazism, swallowing down their emotions and jitterbugging their way to pick up the collective sobriquet of 'the greatest generation', the lot that followed basically invented 'selling out'.

They leave a legacy to the world that includes such atrocities as ponytails on men, the sports jacket/sneaker combination, progressive rock and a fevered support for the doctrine of neoliberalism.

They are the reason you can't afford to buy a house.

They bought them all up when they were going cheap; now they're worth millions.

You ended up paying almost a thousand pounds a month to rent a tiny, windowless shoebox so infested by black mould that you've lost the use of one lung.

All your hard-earned money ended up in the pocket of a baby boomer landlord so utterly devoid of scruples that he tried to pass off the gigantic hole in the kitchen wall as a trompe l'oeil.

There's no money left for food after paying the rent and buying the baccy, so you're forced to eat a mug full of broken noodles and potpourri.

Thanks, Mum and Dad.

Thanks a bunch.

40

At least the peach looks fresh enough, although that could well mean it's not quite ripe enough yet, as hard as a rock and only slightly more palatable.

The true sadness lies in the upturned mouth on the plate, a soggy microwaveable burrito that sits downturned; a grim reminder of your inadequacies in the kitchen and beyond.

It's times like these when you turn to your signed picture of Gregg Wallace for a spot of Wallace solace.

'To the "lovely" Louise, all the best, Gregg' reads the handwritten note scrawled across a glossy portrait of a whimsically nude Wallace sprawled out on a Regency sedan, cheekily scoffing an éclair.

Having the official scrawl of the *MasterChef* ingredients guru would perhaps mean even more to you if your name were Louise.

Perhaps one day you'll change it.

The last woman you went out with (coincidentally named Louise) always told you that Jasper made you sound like a junior Tory minister.

You wonder about the scare quotes around the word 'lovely'.

Was Gregg perhaps being disingenuous when he personalised that photograph?

Was he really expressing genuine human emotion, or had years of lavishing pies, cakes and battered doughnuts with the same affection one would usually reserve for their nearest and dearest left Gregg spent?

You hope not.

The thought of Gregg becoming yet another listless, jaded celebrity produce expert fills you with a terrible sadness.

Buffets are a suspension of the normal rules and conventions of society in the same way a certain type of modern music festival is an excuse for middle-class people to put on a bucket hat, smoke soft drugs, listen to Mumford & Sons and engage in a spot of recreational wife-swapping before returning to their quiet suburban life in Surrey.

I understand chips with everything at a buffet.

It's a declaration that you're a disgusting pig who fully intends to push the lining of your stomach to the limits and get your money's worth by trying to eat a small family-owned restaurant out of business.

I can dig that.

What I can't understand is the mentality of someone going to a Chinese or Indian restaurant and ordering *only* the most anaemic-looking items from the ghetto of English food at the back of the menu.

What sort of person is so genetically hardwired for blandness that they can't even stomach the mildest of kormas?

Perhaps it's the protest vote option for the member of the party who didn't want to go to the Taj Mahal for the mandatory office outing, but was too unpopular or meek, or just plain weird, for their opinion to count.

Chips in the curry house, a reassuring blanket of carbohydrates for the people out there who purse their lips and inwardly tut whenever they come across a name that takes a modicum of effort to pronounce.

That great bunch who call talkSPORT to complain about living in a country they no longer recognise, who bugger off to Spain first chance they get to live on a diet of cooked breakfasts and spite. Who refuse to ever try tapas or to learn the language beyond *dos cervezas, por favor.*

Bad experiences with mushrooms.

They're not limited to first-year philosophy students with chin beards tripping their balls off in their halls of residence, vividly hallucinating that they're on the holodeck from *Star Trek*, stripping off to proclaim there is no such thing as time, all of human existence is occurring simultaneously, and that Eamonn Holmes is the Godhead.

Obviously this is the most common type, happening as it does on average about three times a week in any medium-sized British university.

It's hard to get excited about a plate of rubbery mushrooms and exhausted-looking rice, even from this photograph, where it looks like the shadow of some great Neolithic monument is falling over it.

That or the bedroom door has opened, catching it *in flagrante delicto* with another man's wife. The randy risotto is hurled at the wall by our poor imaginary cuckold shortly before he storms off to sit in his Land Rover for a session of deep animalistic sobbing and Phil Collins on the car stereo.

Some people regard mushrooms as unwelcome intruders, sliming up their plate, when encountered as part of a cooked breakfast, smelling slightly of shameful male discharge.

Others (hippies, druggies, dead stand-up comedians) think they're gifts from the gods that kickstarted the process of evolution from ape to man, that within their fleshy caps they contain all the secrets of the universe, such as why people watch golf on television or the purpose of Vernon Kay.

Bottom line: they work really well in a risotto but can also make you believe you're trapped in Mordor and that your flat is full of goblins.

Be careful.

Cottage cheese must have one of the least interesting origin stories of any cheese.

This fits with its general consumer: uninspired dieters and gym rats happily willing to sacrifice the normal prerequisites for food – pleasant flavour, appetising texture – in favour of high protein content.

Nobody even really cares where the name came from; my cursory research into the subject could only unearth a few lines written by nineteenth-century food writer Uriah Meriwether:

> folk say it was first invented in a cottage or some such similar domicile by the dwellers therein, though all would no doubt be of the thinking that it is a most unenthralling cheese, only to be eaten by those in pursuit of getting shredded and buff and making serious gains.

One bodybuilder I spoke to said that it was called cottage cheese because if you ate enough of it, you would be transformed into a brick shithouse.

However, judging by size of his trap, which looked as if another smaller human being was growing out of his shoulders, and the vast colonies of acne visible on his back, I'd wager he was supplementing his cheese-eating with 'special vitamins'.

One of the things I've learned from being the curator of the most desolate gallery of food photography on the planet is that loneliness and an inability to cook is a truly global phenomenon.

All across this wretched world there are people staring at their microwaves with desperation in their eyes.

The information might be displayed in different languages, but the message is universal:

As you shall eat so shall you die, alone and surrounded by the remnants of ready meals.

That's globalisation for you.

Under every article on a newspaper's website that doesn't directly contain cold hard facts about current events (and even some that do…) there is always some brave standard bearer for news values sagely commenting, 'Is this news?' or, if they're feeling particularly waggish, 'First World Problems'.

Where would we be without these people telling us that lighthearted columns about amusing instances of marital infidelity and restaurant reviews about Soviet-style canteens in Peckham are trivial and undeserving of precious web space?

However, just as McDonald's Happy Meals have become ubiquitous throughout every corner of the globe, so too has the unhappy meal.

In this picture we can see the Egyptian equivalent of eating cold beans from the tin.

In some small way doesn't that make you feel better about your own loneliness?

No?

Well, it would if you weren't so dead inside.

You're keeping alive the memory of your dead dog Ruffio by eating your dinner from his favourite Frisbee.

You're also eating some of the freeze-dried Italian cheese he liked so very much, the pungent powder stuff that looks like your old geography teacher Mr Marston's distinctive off-white dandruff.

Truth be told, you probably shouldn't have been feeding him that stuff. He'd always had a weak stomach and, in all honesty, he really belonged more to your mum, seeing as she was the one who rescued him, washed him, walked him and held his furry little paw as he slipped away to the great canine hereafter.

He'd put up a brave fight, but there were complications following the operation to have that massive ball of compacted fake Parmesan removed from his small intestine.

Mum never found out you were the one feeding Ruffio deadly flakes of the rennet-heavy cheese dust.

She assumed he had figured out how to open the cupboard door, carefully pour out a small amount into his bowl, and then put it neatly back next to the olive oil and the dried porcini.

A sweet woman, your mother, but perhaps guilty of both thinking the best of her only son and overestimating the intelligence of her much-loved, but deeply inbred Yorkshire terrier.

There had been talk before Ruffio died that you would eventually move out.

Eighteen months on and the pipe dream of one day fashioning a bachelor's cocoon out of the remnants of your dead grandmother's furniture in the small crawlspace above where Mum parks her Rover has pretty much gone the way of your other aspirations.

One day, perhaps, you'll have somewhere private to invite Lydia from the Co-op, provided that she doesn't insist on spending some more time alone with the softly spoken Italian Stallion who impressed her so much all those years ago with his knowledge of dried cheeses.

53

From an early age, Bunty has learnt to eat her feelings.

In lieu of loving hugs she turned not to drugs but to the unconditional love of Mr Kipling.

Since birth she's always been the odd one out in her family.

Generally ignored at both the dinner table and in the street in favour of the family's black Labrador Michael, Bunty has grown accustomed to her mother telling strangers and acquaintances alike that she was rescued under dead of night from one of Ceausescu's infamous orphanages.

She hadn't; she was 100 per cent homegrown and organic. But for her mother the tall tale considerably enlivened the prospect of being parent to a little girl widely regarded as a very dull child.

Perhaps it was because Bunty did not care for skiing lessons, tennis club, trips with Nanny to the farmers' market or any of the other typical middle-class substitutes for love and affection.

Over the years, Bunty has clad herself in a heavy armour of adipose tissue.

Now is the time for change. Gone are the lemon slices and Battenberg segments.

In their place a tasteless chicken, vegetable and organic rice mush.

The pure joylessness of her food is melting away the fat just as surely as her unloving mother's insistence on forcing her to attend ballet classes for three years put it there.

There's a certain brand of overly seasoned tortilla chip that purports to be cheese-flavoured, the eating of which will stain your fingers worse than a twenty-a-day unfiltered Camels habit.

They're not without their charms, although sustained consumption will mark your mouth and make it appear that your digits have been intimate with an Oompa Loompa.

Perhaps you ate them, or a similarly powdery crisp, at school and used to wipe your fingers down a schoolmate's back, marking them out as the recipient of some unexpected 'beats'.

They do make surprisingly good nachos, though.

Not in this case, it would seem. These are awful barrel-scraping nachos clearly made by someone either very high or very desperate, who has emptied most of a bottle of jalapeño relish over some burnt chips and flicked a laughable quantity of Cheddar over the result. Laughable, that Cheddar.

However, when the stars align and you have one or more of the essential ingredients to make nachos – cheese, for example – then even at their laziest they can be most pleasant to enjoy in front of a marathon binge of *Storage Hunters*.

You've had arguments in the past with your friend Ian about which is the superior storage box show.

On one occasion, the two of you nearly came to blows over his repeated insistence that *Storage Wars* is superior by merit of it being the first of the two to come out; it is the original and therefore the best.

A ludicrous line of thinking that you thought you'd shut down with the classic *Godfather* vs *Godfather II* argument, which he then insisted was about sequels, not rip-offs.

After that you lost your temper and told him you'd never really loved him.

In time, nachos mended that bridge.

58

The plate reads 'BREAKFAST, LUNCH, DINNER', which makes it a dangerous trigger for those of us who feel our lives are stuck in an endless, unchanging loop.

Look at that plate. Go on, look at what's on it.

Do you have any idea what it is?

Is it couscous?

Could it be egg?

Surely it's not porridge?

Wait, is that grey stuff in the meat?

Not sure?

Neither am I.

That's the point.

It could be breakfast, lunch or dinner.

It's probably been all three at various points during the week; time has no meaning anymore when you're stuck alone in a small box devoid of any human interaction, breathing in your own stench day after day until even you're sick of you.

It's so quiet when you're in the flat all on your own and the upstairs neighbour isn't having loud, angry sex.

Turn up the television as loud as you can, it still won't drown out the reproachful voice in your head that's saying, 'Fuck's sake, Gary, what have you done with your life?'

You find you're getting into work earlier and earlier and leaving later, even though you're doing less work. Your job could be done by any one of the less intelligent primates if they had a basic level of Microsoft Office experience and attended fire marshal training.

No, work now consists of looking at dating websites, adding pictures of hamburgers to your Pinterest, and trying not to think about the empty flat you go home to.

Final demands travel through Gillian's letterbox with the same depressing regularity as a stony-faced commuter making their daily train ride into the heart of darkness.

That Grim Reaper of the destitute and needy known as Austerity has its bony fingers wrapped tightly around her neck and it will not let go.

Gillian laments the fact her children's clothes are woefully out of date and constantly in need of repair, that the zero-hours contract she's on offers nothing in the way of job security, and that many nights she goes hungry so as to ensure her kids get a decent meal.

A dismal heap of the day before yesterday's potatoes and a small pile of salt gathered from the dried-out tears of her desolate offspring.

Gillian awaits the sound of the postman's arrival with trepidation.

Will today's post bring yet more threats from energy providers determined to see Gillian and her children freeze to death this winter if she is unable to stump up the cash she owes?

Perhaps it will be the standard shower of takeaway leaflets on the doormat cruelly mocking her with deals she cannot afford.

No, today brings none of the above.

Instead, lands a letter from the Government telling her she's now ineligible for benefits unless she agrees to place one or more of her progeny in a workhouse.

This is the food porn that Fred and Rose West might have produced if they'd dedicated their energies towards photographing their meals and blogging recycled Elizabeth David recipes, rather than participating in the wholesale slaughter of the innocent.

It's a seedy, small-town answer to the fancy food photography you'd find in a copy of *Good Food* magazine, a seedy Polaroid plucked from the pages of Readers' Wives held up in comparison to a classical Greek nude.

The dingy bedroom setting chosen by this artist of dinner-time sleaze only adds to the uncomfortable gonzo vibe, with the plate looking like it's been stolen from a retirement home kitchen and clashing horribly with the sickly stripes of bed sheets that have time travelled into the present from a 1970s Robin Askwith film.

There's a real sense that this is the handiwork of a suburban sex offender, the creep next door conveniently forgetting to tie his dressing gown when emptying the bins on a Sunday morning, all in the sordid hope of 'accidentally' exposing himself to a disgusted universe.

A dark and unsettling image, much like the kind of blurred picture a certain type of young male might keep on his phone as a sexual trophy. The queasy perspective no doubt a result of the photographer being perched awkwardly at the foot of his bed.

He looms over the hotdogs like that one suspect PE teacher from your schooldays, insistently checking that everyone is indeed taking their showers and not still wearing their pants, the faintest trace of a leer on an otherwise inscrutable face.

Normally the letters spell out 'ennui' but today there's only one 'n'.

Angered by your father's refusal to carry on subsidising your chosen lifestyle as a cabaret compère you've chosen to chastise him via the medium of potatoes fashioned into extremely crude characters.

It's certainly a loaded word.

Controversial, even, if you're an American or something.

The incorrect use of it could result in a lot of hand-wringing *Guardian* think-pieces and self-righteous Twitter outrage.

Depending, of course, on who's using the word and whether or not there's anything sexier going on in the news, such as a pop singer being accused of cultural appropriation or a politician sending pictures of his gnarled old penis to a made-up woman.

There are no two ways about it: this is indeed a *problematic* dinner.

Some people simply do not like the word 'cunt'.

Some people can't abide breaded turkey escallops and thick-cut oven chips.

Sometimes these dislikes intersect and you're left with someone who would unreservedly disapprove of Bernard Matthews, the cunt.

Is it perhaps a bit harsh to extend these words to your dad, even if he is threatening to cut the purse strings and have you put aside the top hat and greasepaint to return to a career in town planning?

Definitely, but it's the only way he'll pay any attention to you.

Not all dimly lit meals for one are eaten by sad single people with severe emotional problems.

Sometimes they're prepared by sad married people with severe emotional problems and teenage children with even more severe emotional problems.

Ungrateful teenage children who take pictures of the meal that their tired and stressed-out parents dutifully assembled for them and then send the photographic evidence of their love for them to a complete stranger to be ridiculed in print.

It's a sick, sad, screwed-up world we live in.

One in which entitled teenagers with ridiculous fringes, ludicrous lip rings and god-awful taste in music can barely muster enough energy to look away from their Stupid Sexy YouTube to sneer derisively at their parents' honest home cooking.

Then sigh, exasperated by their parents' very existence, and go back to gawping at other teenagers bleating trite inanities into a webcam and trying to sell them acne cream. Other teenagers who are, at least, more successful than the feckless offspring of these poor hardworking parents – despite having even more ridiculous fringes and stupider lip rings – waving their hands around on camera, being 'wacky' and talking with an inflection so rising it's in danger of leaving the earth's atmosphere.

Despite all their contrived zaniness and irritating youthful exuberance, these video blogging stars would probably never even consider 'anonymously' sending pictures of their mum's cooking to a man in his thirties compiling a book on mediocre food.

Shame on you, anonymous teen, shame on you!

Rhiannon scavenged this lonely offering after a long day spent working in a sandwich shop for a minimum wage and minimum respect.

By the time she eats it alone in abject silence the lettuce is warm and limp, the mayonnaise has congealed, and the chunks of roasted chicken are sweating like a 1970s DJ under cross-examination.

If she were honest though, free food isn't the real reason Rhiannon is doing this job.

Nor is it the money that keeps her coming back to the Snack Shack every weekend. Rhiannon knows full well she could be earning significantly more and getting some much-needed fresh air by standing in the city centre for the day clutching a big sign labelled 'GOLF SALE'.

No, there is another reason she tolerates the low pay and constant stench of cucumber on her hands.

There is one customer who comes in every Saturday morning after football practice, who orders the same roast beef and horseradish baguette every week, and whose striking mane of raven-black hair might well have reminded Rhiannon of a young David Essex, had she been born many, many years previously.

Every week she prays that this will be the day she receives something more than a muttered thanks, a smile, a wink, a sneeze.

God, now she thinks about the potential exchange of fluids it would involve, *especially* a sneeze.

69

Herman cakes are made from a chain of Lovecraftian, semi-immortal yeast that was historically passed around by middle-aged German women before *The Secret* was translated and they all got into book groups instead.

They're described as 'friendship' cakes, which perhaps precludes most of the people reading this book from enjoying them.

The cakes mirror real-life friendship by being a burden you'd really rather give up on but to which you return grudgingly out of a sense of obligation.

Richard's mum passed some on to his girlfriend, who baked and subsequently froze one each year until their relationship crumbled away like so much stale cake.

As the weeks went by and Richard waited out the lease on the small terraced flat they had once shared, his thoughts often turned to Herman the cake, sitting there all alone in the dark and cold, frozen solid like Walt Disney's head.

During their relationship he had felt that a collaborative yeast-sharing exercise was somehow sinister, that there was something distinctly unsavoury about the whole process, but before he could leave his flat of broken dreams Richard's abhorrence of waste compelled him to eat his way through the contents of the freezer.

Richard wakes Herman from stasis, puts him in the microwave, scrapes out the dregs of some six-month-old Asda Smart Price ice cream and drowns the Teutonic dessert in golden syrup.

The sickly-sweet treat eaten in lieu of a healthy and nutritious meal brings a single solitary tear to Richard's eye.

Seconds later, 'She's Gone' by Hall & Oates comes on the radio and the lone tear gives way to a steady flood.

Geoff comes from Coventry, a town all but destroyed by German bombers during the Second World War.

Geoff would never say it out loud, but after a long day of being ignored by everyone, on returning to a cold house and a dirty kitchen he sometimes utters a silent prayer asking for the bombs to once more rain down upon the Midlands town as he peers into his combination fridge-freezer.

It has become an involuntary reaction, much like the shudder of dread and accompanying hot prickle of anger he experienced when the telephone rang and he was forced into yet another needless confrontation with an inarticulate young man trying to talk him into a PPI refund.

Looking inside, he sees a loaf of bread and four value-range fish fingers.

Geoff has taken to freezing his bread after losing one loaf too many to the insidious green mould. He would become so enraged when he discovered his bread had broken bad that he'd bypass the usual wall-punching stage of his food rage and go straight to the bitter sobbing and strangled howling.

Then Geoff remembers there is someone in his flat whom he can rely upon, someone who always had his back and who looks out for his best interests.

The remote control.

Resting in its own little groove on the arm of his recliner.

It would never criticise Geoff for wanting to stay in and watch Jason Statham films, or ditch him for a ponytail-wearing Pilates instructor named Rafael.

You wake up on a Wednesday morning in January, naked and wet in the bathtub of your unheated flat.

The abrasive chemicals in the cheap Polish beer you were guzzling the night before act like antifreeze in your blood, keeping you from freezing to death and, you suspect, are gradually changing the structure of your DNA.

You figured out a while ago that you are just as competent doing your job with a crippling hangover as you are stone-cold sober.

Perhaps you are even a little better, certainly less inhibited and willing to take chances, when you turn up half-drunk.

The only downside is your body's complete inability to function when pumped full of strong lager, hence often waking at 7am to find you have spent the evening marinating in a shallow pool of recycled beer. Washing off the secretions of the previous night you leave, late as usual, to spend the day at work being patronised by your much younger manager.

Returning from yet another inconsequential day spent selling rubbish to idiots, you are gripped by panic when you remember that you failed to remove the drumsticks from the freezer.

Smashing the frozen chicken legs out of the packet with a hammer, you try to defrost the trio of limbs in the microwave.

This is a fool's errand; nobody knows how to use the defrost function on a microwave.

Nobody.

In desperation you submerge the poultry in boiling-hot water.

It seems to work as the flesh becomes warmer, less resistant to your prodding.

Half-cooked and covered in bobbles of white fat, you decide it's safe to stick it in the oven.

And then this.

This is what you have.

75

Can a bowl of food be reproachful?

Maria certainly thinks so as she looks down at her sullen fishcakes and morose mashed potatoes.

They remind her of her teenage son who spent many an evening glaring at Maria across the kitchen table with undisguised contempt as she served him a lovingly prepared home-cooked meal.

It wasn't long before his father easily bought the fickle boy's love with a PlayStation and the little shit went to live with him in Jersey.

Maria had thought she was accustomed to this level of betrayal, but it still stings to have come a distant third in her son's affection, after *Call of Duty* and a steady diet of takeaways.

She places the miserable-looking food next to her on the Italian leather sofa she had insisted on having as part of the divorce settlement.

Maria hates it; it doesn't go with any of the other furniture and she suspects it to be the cause of the strange rash on her arms.

Her ex-husband, however, had loved it. Possibly more than his son. Knowing this made the custody arrangements slightly easier to swallow.

Unlike the sullen fishcake stuck in Maria's throat, causing fleeting panic as she entertains the prospect of choking to death alone on a sofa she detests before she dislodges it with a self-administered approximation of the Heimlich manoeuvre.

Martin compensates for his inherently dull personality by wearing extremely loud shirts, reciting popular comedy catchphrases and being aggressively and relentlessly cheerful towards both his co-workers and the unfortunate strangers he encounters while out and about.

Forced jollity keeps the gnawing demons of self-doubt at bay, at least during the day when he is bathed in the glow of the call centre's fluorescent strip lighting.

At night it's a different story.

Exhausted by his constant performance of what he perceives to be a normal human being, Martin barely has the energy to pour a can of beans into a bowl of undercooked pasta.

Draped over a sofa fifty shades of beige he shovels forkfuls of the tasteless stodge into his crowded mouth.

The neon pink shirt covered in little stitched flamingoes that Martin wore to work sits crumpled on the floor, a large sweat stain under each armpit.

It is garish and sad at the same time, like a velvet painting of a crying clown or a condolence card from Clintons.

Martin recalls the day's forced banter, in particular the haunting expression of despair on his colleague's face as he gently reprimanded him, using some lines borrowed from *Little Britain*, for failing to reach his weekly sales targets.

Martin knows he's a terrible person but, like the painfully bland food he forces into his mouth night after night, he is powerless to change.

Jeremy looks at the cold sausage rolls on his excessively labelled side plate and lets out a deep sigh.

He's forgotten to make a real meal for himself again, deliberately placing the two pastries on a small plate in the hope that his eyes will fool his stomach into thinking he has eaten a decent-sized dish of food.

The little side plate is his favourite piece of crockery.

That side plate is arguably his avatar in the kitchen; the one item that best represents what he is all about.

Small, not particularly attractive and with an annoying habit of repeating itself. Never the main attraction, it exists and that is about it.

Jeremy feels a strange kinship with the budget kitchenware sitting in front of him.

They are both on the periphery of their own lives, jealously looking on while bigger and brasher plates are heaped high with potatoes and covered with life's sweet gravy.

It is fitting that the neglected side plate is the only piece of crockery Jeremy has left.

His ex-girlfriend took the rest when she moved in with Jeremy's ex-best friend.

He had questioned why they needed all of his plates; he received only a withering stare in response.

Jeremy sits with the little side plate and his sausage rolls and thinks about visiting Matalan for some new plates. He starts to feel a bit depressed.

SIDEPLATE • SIDEPLATE • SIDEPLATE • SIDEPLATE • SIDEPLATE • SIDEPLATE • SIDEPLATE • SIDEPLATE

People say there's no colour in my diet, but it's simply not true.

This plate of food encompasses the whole spectrum – from burnt chip brown to mayo white.

There's no need to be ashamed of living a white-bread existence.

Fancy food isn't for everyone. I mean, everyone has to eat, but being *into* food?

It's like being really *into* sex, being one of those sex people, isn't it?

Going to orgies, reading sex manuals, buying expensive salt from Tibet: all much of a muchness.

Sex people, food people, two sides of the same coin really.

Surely there's more to life than shagging and eating? If you're a thirty-seven-year-old virgin with malfunctioning taste buds and a plunging hairline then the answer, hopefully, is yes.

Otherwise, the outlook is decidedly bleak.

There's so much snobbery about food that I don't understand.

I don't get judgemental with people just because they don't know anything about *Doctor Who*, despite the fact it's legacy television that should be taught in schools.

You can eat chips every day and live perfectly healthily for years.

I should know; I've been doing it since I was twelve.

Okay, I collapse at work roughly every two to three months, my face is flakier than a Ginsters pasty that's been reheated in the oven, and my body odour smells like a grease trap.

But I'm not dead yet.

Alone in a world where only the potatoes have eyes for you.

Where are all the good times?

Like your hair, they're long gone.

You remember the first time you heard the old analogy 'like a pair of bald men fighting over a comb'.

You laughed at the time because you had a full head of hair.

Now you're bald and you find that you're fighting with another bald man.

Not over a comb, but for the affections of a woman named Stella, whom you both met on an over-forties dating website.

Stella is the one glimmer of hope in a moribund existence. She is large and dimpled and beaming. When she visits for tea and biscuits she illuminates your rancid bachelor pit and makes it seem almost bearable.

You suspect your love rival Ian (also bald, accountant, cocky) of having ulterior motives.

Stella is sitting on a large inheritance, financially speaking, although you suspect her ample buttocks to also be a gift from her mother.

The thought that she might choose Ian over you fills you with dread. Love is a battlefield; your kitchen table is the front line.

You're certain that the way to Stella's heart is not through her chest cavity but via her stomach.

That's why tonight is so important. If this mashed swede doesn't do it...

You can't entertain doubt.

It's going to happen.

It *has* to happen.

The Ians of this world can't win.

This is a picture that brings to mind what might have happened had Bill Cosby been violently sick all down the front of one of his famously shit, yet very expensive sweaters.

Sweaters which are now particularly popular with desperate young men involved in the act of 'peacocking'.

For those of you – whether casually flicking through this book in the reduced section at Poundland, or perusing it with increasing disinterest while at home sitting on the toilet, having received it as an unwanted Christmas gift – unfamiliar with the term 'peacocking', it refers to a technique used by beta males to attract women without any need for a well-defined personality or the ability to converse.

The thinking is that by dressing in loud and obnoxious clothes the 'peacock' will instantly be the centre of attention, enticing a bevy of lovelies to come and marvel at his neon green suspenders, *South Park* necktie and rakish fedora.

Much like real-life peacocks do in the wild (minus the suspenders; peacocks don't wear trousers).

Once lured in by the bright colours and dazzling decorative rhinestones, the disorientated woman will easily fall prey to the peacock's mysterious charm and skills at close-up magic and contact juggling.

This is the theory, at least.

In practice it tends to lead to a lot of men being turned away from clubs by bouncers worried that they've got a colourblind sex offender on their hands.

Men who go home and play their ukuleles and eat garish food with a child's fork.

Men you desperately don't want your young son to grow into, yet suspect, deep down, that it's already too late.

Imagine getting microwaved vegan macaroni and cheese wrong.

Go on, imagine experiencing that level of ineptitude.

That's worse than failing your cycling proficiency test because you were too much of a coward to take your hands off the handlebars for ten seconds to signal left.

There was your dad looking on, mournfully shaking his head, unwilling to admit to himself that the loudly sobbing eleven-year-old going round in circles on a girl's bike was really his son.

If only your dear old Dad could see you now, the unfortunate fruit of his loins an artfully dishevelled, fully bearded man-child struggling to cope with entry-level convenience food.

He'd have suggested you fry a steak, only for you to meekly tell him you're a vegan. You can imagine the sound of the sigh he'd emit, like the muted howl of a mournful breeze on a British beach in winter.

It's probably for the best that he left that Sunday afternoon to go look at power tools and never returned home.

His eyes might have burst with sadness to see you updating the 'interested in' section on your Facebook to 'pansexual', forty minutes after you read about it for the first time.

They'd have overflowed with salt tears after witnessing you backpedal on the drastic change in lifestyle after you'd tried to explain the term to your befuddled grandmother.

It clearly didn't register, as to this day she keeps her kitchen cupboards locked when you're around for fear you'll interfere with her Le Creuset.

You'll have to take it on faith that there is a smattering of cheese between those two decidedly flat-looking tortillas.

A Mexican quesadilla made with North Korean ration-sized portions of good old mild English Cheddar.

That's what Anthony calls fusion cooking.

He is working his way through the cuisines of the world, one meal kit at a time, but like the magazines of his childhood that promised the excitement of building a dinosaur week by week at an excruciatingly slow pace, he seems to be missing a vital piece.

Anthony is undeterred. Consistent failure doesn't make him any less eager to try and broaden his horizons. He feels that eventually he'll get it right; that he'll find the perfect dish and everything will fall into place shortly afterwards.

In the meantime, there are obstacles to overcome. An accident with a cheese grater, several hours spent in A&E, shredded thumb in the fajitas.

Anthony considers these character-defining moments. He'd not shied away from doing his share of the cooking when Mum left.

Granted, his dad had begged him to stop after a particularly vicious bout of food poisoning left him soiled and ashamed in front of the Swindon office, but that was by the by. Anthony is a grown man now, a modern man, and if he's to have any hope of finding someone to share his life with then he must be able to pull his weight in the kitchen.

Lentils are highly politicised pulses.

They're often used pejoratively alongside muesli as cultural shorthand to disparage *Guardian* readers, the implication being that they're enjoyed by sandal-wearing university lecturers who still believe in the power of protest and who feel guilt about things.

That's a highly offensive stereotype, mainly because it's so outdated.

Those people gave up on the *Guardian* years ago.

Now it's staffed entirely by insufferable twenty-somethings with very important opinions giving their hot takes on reaching peak beard, normcore and culturally appropriative cereal cafés.

Luckily, lentils nowadays are for everyone, not just hippies.

Take the person who cooked up this plate. They don't care about anything.

Syria, gender inequality, fracking. Couldn't give a fuck.

They know nothing really matters, least of all their own comfort and happiness.

That's why they eat lentils: they know they don't deserve any better.

Greet every day with a 'meh' and shrug your shoulders at injustice and barbarism.

Look at a picture of a funny cat and forget to feed the one you've got.

Your apathy extends to the kitchen and lentils are your karmic reward.

Don't pretend you enjoy them.

Don't pretend.

Derek has long given up on ever being an inspirational teacher and is focused entirely on waiting out the two years left before he can take early retirement.

Every day is worse than the one before.

The sound of children's voices like nails dragged across a blackboard, interminable meetings which last longer than forever, mountain upon mountain of turgid essays that parrot what he said in class but still manage to get it all completely bloody wrong.

Despite having a mild allergy to the skin of the fruit, Derek forces himself to eat half the apple.

He is so very hungry.

He can feel his throat tighten slightly but he presses on, afraid that he might pass out from hunger otherwise.

Everyone had been required to stay late for parents' evening and the promised sandwiches never transpired.

Unsurprising, really – the headteacher is what Derek's dad would have called a spiv.

Derek calls him far worse.

The only refreshments on offer are a bowl of fruit on the turn and the fairy cakes made in a Year Nine food technology class he had ended up covering because Mrs Newby was busy in a clinic somewhere getting through the DTs.

Derek ate three of those cakes despite being fully aware that the children never washed their hands.

He had his suspicions that Peter Newton had drooled into his cake mix.

That boy had the worst case of cold sores he'd ever seen on a fourteen-year-old.

Derek makes a mental note to book an appointment with his GP and gingerly begins eating his fourth fairy cake.

Life is an ocean of bleakness scattered across which are islands of pure horror.

Most of the time we're simply wading through the shallow waters of misery.

A Friday night spent scraping cat diarrhoea from the skirting boards, an evening of ITV programming hosted by Vernon Kay, three hours cornered in the pub by a man with an encyclopaedic knowledge of football-conference statistics and no desire to talk about anything else.

Nineteen pence budget-brand noodles and the shavings of a piquant chilli Cheddar you bought by mistake; cutting corners with the food shopping so you can afford a wrap of mephedrone, should things get truly desperate.

The bare minimum of food required to sufficiently line your stomach before subjecting it to all-out chemical warfare in the form of super-strength lager.

The waves of tedium and mundanity may wash you ashore onto one of the rocky outcrops of life-altering terror.

Perhaps you'll awake missing a leg, or in a burning flat, or with a battered and bloody corpse in the bathtub.

Is it wrong that secretly you yearn for something out of the ordinary to happen?

Even if it's something really bad, something truly awful, anything would be better than suffering through the tedium of another night spent shovelling bland stodge into your gaping maw while watching Z-list celebrities and their relatives get straightforward questions dead wrong on *All Star Family Fortunes*.

Maybe it's time to break out the meow-meow, only a half-teaspoon or so.

Just enough to give the noodles a kick.

There's mayonnaise on the pastrami and jam on the cheese.

The song in your heart has a catchy yet sweetly melancholic refrain and from your window you can see a flock of starlings pirouetting through the sky in a magical murmuration.

It's a crisp autumn day and you're struck by a pleasant wistfulness that starts in your nether regions and works its way all the way up to your brain.

Yes, you're definitely on drugs.

That's why you've been rubbing your head in the same spot for an hour and a half and that's also why it felt so good.

It's obviously why you've forgotten how to make a sandwich.

Don't worry, though – it's all okay.

As long as nobody's coming over today, what does it matter how you spend your Sunday afternoon?

Oh.

Your parents? And your *grandparents*?

This could be bad.

Maybe you should think about how best to arrange your face so it doesn't look like you're on drugs.

Yes. Stand in front of the mirror and practise looking normal.

And get rid of that sandwich.

If your nanna sees that, well, she'll know.

She always knows.

Dwayne is watching a documentary all about the lives of the great French chefs when he comes across a fascinating recipe involving a chicken cooked inside a pig's bladder.

The sight of the porcine piss sack stuffed full of truffles and shallots before being manually inflated by a gasping Parisian masterchef causes his stomach to rumble with the righteous fury of a man shortchanged by his newsagent.

It's inspiring to see consummate professionals at work and a thrill to bear witness to the human ingenuity that would think to cook a chicken inside a pig.

Throughout his life, Dwayne has been made to feel like he didn't have any good ideas.

During group work at school he was always in charge of 'cutting out' and 'sticking on'.

At work he had been told he needed to get to grips with the box before he could attend a training session on thinking outside of it.

Wandering out to the shed, he rummages around a dusty brown box full of his old toys until he finds a semi-inflated football that bears the face of Peter Beardsley.

For many years it had occupied a small pillow next to his own.

Dwayne takes the ball and widens the hole in the inflatable, situated as it is in the middle of Beardsley's left eye, just enough so that a frozen stick of cod can pass through.

This is to be his pig's bladder; this is to be his shining moment.

There are so many things you can do with potatoes, but right now you feel all you deserve is to boil a couple of them whole, maybe throw in some of yesterday's cabbage, and be done with it.

Chips and mash, they're for brighter, happier days.

Those blissful days where you'd sit on the hill overlooking the Tesco car park and watch a strong wind blow the unattended trolleys into the sides of the parked cars.

The summer nights of your youth when while returning home from an evening of soft drugs and drinking you'd steal bottles of milk from the doorsteps of people who naively supported their local dairies instead of shopping at the supermarket like everyone else.

People who prefer their potatoes to have a few eyes and the odd patch of dirt.

People who appreciate a reasonable amount of authenticity without going mental over it and trading the rosebeds for a cabbage patch.

You'd like to look at potatoes the way those people do, heart-shaped dauphinoise with a well-matched red in their eyes.

But you're not that sort of person. Not anymore. You're not even lumpy mash these days.

The truth is you're spending more time washing potatoes than you are washing yourself.

When was the last time you got out of bed before *Loose Women* was on?

Those days aren't coming back.

She's not coming back.

Might as well draw a face on a potato and rest its little head on the pillow next to yours.

That's as good as it's going to get.

He had planned to take the perfect mashed-potato selfie but no matter how many times Ryan adjusted the angle of his phone he still kept managing to cut his head off.

It had taken a considerable amount of time to cover his fish fingers with the potato and pea purée and he was proud of the edible citadel sitting at his table. Ryan would have liked his beaming face in the shot.

It doesn't matter all that much, though, as he is an expert with Photoshop.

In fact, Ryan has spent the last six months digitally manipulating himself into a variety of different photographs, all of which make it look as if he is in a long-term relationship.

Ryan has been going through something of a life-long dry spell, romantically speaking, and he reasons that he might appear more attractive to prospective mates if he is able to reassure them that he has consistently been in the vicinity of a consenting woman.

The photo collages are so realistic that they might conceivably have tricked his friends on Facebook, had Ryan not dreamed just that little bit too big and chosen popular Barbadian songstress Rihanna as his bogus paramour.

It looks as though he will be spending the foreseeable future without someone to share his mashed potato mansion of many rooms.

Cabbage with nacho cheese dip over it is not the same thing as coleslaw.

As much as you might try to convince yourself that the simulacrum of food sitting in front of you is a real side dish you're sadly labouring under a delusion.

It only makes matters worse when Linda walks in on you staring dejectedly at your plastic lunchbox full of fauxslaw and asks you what you have there.

'Cold sores? Did you hear that, Mike? Deborah's got cold sores! Been kissing Gavin again, Debs?'

Your meek protestations go unheard.

You quite clearly said 'coleslaw'.

Your face becomes the exact same shade as the red cabbage in your awful salad.

Thoughts of tipping the emergency eyewash from the staff kitchen first-aid kit into a cup of Linda's smug-looking instant cappuccino race through your head.

It's odourless and tasteless and the right amount in a hot beverage can make someone heave their guts out.

There's a reason so many people in the office have been laid out with mystery twenty-four-hour stomach viruses.

Society with its rules and acceptable behaviours prohibits what you would consider a reasonable response to Linda's awfulness. However, there exists in this world a natural justice and it has given us certain tools we can use to tip the scales in our favour.

Namely, an assortment of laxatives and mild poisons we can place in various foodstuffs to smite our enemies and leave them expelling rusty water in the office toilets.

Pretty much anything goes with a decent red.

A stick of mozzarella covered in peach jam.

Crippling doubt and insecurity.

Prank telephone calls at four in the morning to the man your children call 'Daddy'. Treacherous swine.

Sure, why not?

Red, red wine.

It helps you forget the heartless woman you met at a UB40 gig several years and trouser sizes earlier. Back when they called them 'gigs', back when UB40 were Britain's premier live reggae act.

It was a UB40 song that you chose for the first dance at your wedding, or possibly Simply Red. You forget; it was something from around that time.

Perhaps Chris Rea, now you come to think about it. It's difficult to remember after so many glasses of wine. Doesn't matter now. You know what she danced to with the new chap: M People, 'Moving On Up'.

Barbed reference to the fact she is now with a man who bought a new Jaguar every year.

Probably shouldn't call him up again, old boy, not since the police had words. Everyone was very understanding.

Still, he had looked so smug... you'd love to have had the last word for once.

No, bad idea. Best not to—

Too late now, it's ringing.

'And, another thing, Ian, what the fuck did you do with my Simply Red records?

'Hello?

'Hello?'

Adequately assembling a passable pasta sauce is one of the key thresholds of adulthood. If it's red and there's a few fusilli floating around somewhere in it, you're halfway there. Throw in a mangled red pepper and you're laughing.

This bowl of pasta, however, reeks of deep disconsolation with the act of growing up.

It's as if the cook knows that maturity is a sham, a conscious contrivance involving giving up denim for corduroy, slogan shirts for cable knits, and pie-eyed optimism for a complete absence of hope.

Growing up means giving up on your dreams of learning to dance modern jazz, getting a job in Human Resources, and pretending that what you do every day isn't inherently worthless.

Growing up means fending for yourself by emptying a tin of chopped tomatoes into a saucepan and telling yourself that it's all going to work out somehow.

But you know, deep down, that as with your weak attempts at a ragù you're only passing as an adult human being.

A feeble mask made from a folded paper plate and a few shells of broken pasta. Two poorly punched eyeholes through which your tears are quite apparent.

Beer-can chicken – by now everyone knows that it's massively overrated and has a negligible effect on the taste of the meat.

This year it's all about using the shopping-bag technique and making park-boozer chicken.

You take a factory-farmed bird that's cheap and has led a life of unimaginable torment and you stuff its dead, naked body into a supermarket carrier bag.

One of the flimsy opaque ones from Tesco is probably best for your purposes, although other flimsy bags unable to carry the average adult's honest nightly booze ration are also available.

Now, marinate the bird in white cider, the stronger the better.

As a general rule anything with the words 'diamond', 'frosty' or 'lightning' in the title is a safe bet.

Don't forget to throw in a few handfuls of rolling tobacco, something high tar and liable to stain both tooth and moustache is preferable.

Stick it in a hot oven until your kitchen smells like the unwelcome embrace of an over-affectionate crustie at a free summer festival.

Take it out and marvel at a world of flavour previously only known to those men in dishevelled suits, briefcases full of Special Brew, sitting in silence on park benches getting quietly wrecked while their families think they're at the office still gainfully employed.

Get sick in a bin.

Repeat as necessary.

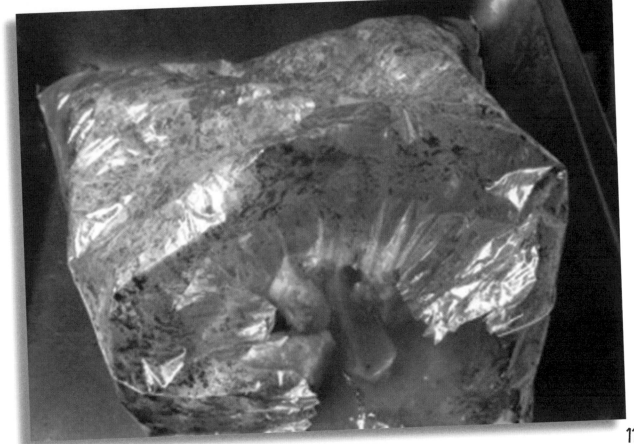

Hugo always told anyone who'd listen that it was better to fail gloriously than to pass with mediocrity.

It was how he'd managed to end his last relationship after drunkenly berating his girlfriend's nice earnest friends about trickledown economics, loudly advocating a flat-rate tax and attempting to punch a bespectacled man named Clive, who was wearing a keffiyeh.

Another evening that finished prematurely with Hugo rolling around on a pub carpet, grappling with himself while moderate drinkers looked on in horror.

Goodbye to a personal best relationship length of seven weeks. Another glorious failure.

The sad truth is that Hugo is a deeply troubled Tory, quite possibly a racist, almost certainly an alcoholic.

The carnage followed him home and into the kitchen. Every meal seems to be a carrot's vision of hell, the spirit of Bosch summoned in a burnt saucepan on a Saturday night in Surrey.

Hugo dreams of himself in a helicopter, 'Ride Of The Valkyries' blaring out on massive speakers, fields of carrots beneath him cowering as he obliterates a pastoral idyll with napalm.

Napalm, which in Hugo's hands now looks to be simply a bottle of sunflower oil, clung to like a lover by a drunk in a burning kitchen.

This will be the year you develop arms that bulge like a sock filled with walnuts.

The pull-up bar was delivered to reception at work last Tuesday.

You could have sworn that the extremely attractive temporary receptionist looked impressed when you picked it up like it weighed nothing, sucking in your stomach and telling her in great detail about your plans to spend the summer getting ripped.

The peals of her laughter as you walked back to the office confirmed it: you'd become instantly more desirable merely by purchasing that wonderful, wonderful bar.

As was the case when deciding which new generation games console to buy, you've done your research. The great PlayStation vs Xbox debate had eaten up hours and hours of time at work as you covertly conducted painstaking research comparing memory and processing speeds, and lots of other things you didn't really understand but which seemed very important.

This time it's a lot more straightforward.

You don't need to spend all day on bodybuilding forums or looking at big lads with their shirts off to know what it's all about, although you have and it's helped.

There's a cheat code, a shortcut you can take to having a chiselled physique, and this time you know the magic word.

It's protein.

Eat enough of it and you'll have muscles to spare.

It's easy too – it comes in tubs and you can get free delivery when you buy online.

It even comes in chocolate flavour.

Imagine that receptionist's face when it turns up at work this week.

She'll be dead impressed.

Sitting down to eat a heaped pile of garlic mash, Rachel sighs involuntarily.

Those are empty calories for an empty heart.

Love left Rachel's kitchen some time ago.

Even the sight of her favourite bowl staring back at her, the one with the twee little teapots (tweepots) enjoying their teapot dance, fails to raise the customary smile.

Where once there had been the sound of her voice talking to her partner, now there is merely silence.

Where once she had enjoyed telling her ex-boyfriend Alan that she was allergic to whatever he cooked, now she dines alone.

It isn't that she misses him.

She had been meaning, when the time was right, to shed him along with all the other embarrassing habits she'd picked up while at university, like voting Liberal Democrat and wearing Ugg boots.

Rachel hadn't expected him to do the ditching first, but apparently Alan found someone who liked fennel in their salads, who didn't mind that he had given up a successful career in the City to spend his time helping the needy and describing rainbows to blind children; who didn't covertly stab him in the leg with a fork under the table when he was being boring at dinner parties.

On reflection, maybe she did miss him.

At that moment, staring at her tweepot bowl, Rachel decides to send him a rather revealing selfie.

Perhaps this new girlfriend might inadvertently spot it and there'd be a little trouble in paradise for Alan and bloody Mother Teresa.

You had to admit that it stung when your housemates changed your OkCupid profile picture to a close-up of one of your less successful soups.

You received a fair few concerned messages advising you to see a genitourinary specialist and a string of unsolicited pictures that looked like blurred close-ups of a miniature kielbasa.

Sadly, it was the most attention you'd had in years and the reason why you were now sitting next to a tall, intently staring stranger on the last bus home, a bowl of broth perched precariously on your lap.

It's a murky world of first-course perversions you're swimming in but it's impossible to get out of it now.

Soon you'll become the notorious good-time girl who can only get their rocks off in the vicinity of chowder.

Not the blizzard of champagne cocktails and theatre trips you had imagined for yourself when you innocently signed up for online matchmaking.

How could you have known the internet was a festering swamp of damaged people consumed by soup-related paraphilias?

You thought it was a happy place for looking at pictures of funny cats and ordering pizza without having to speak to working-class people. But it's a portal of evil and always has been, and now this is your life, one sordid soup encounter after another.

121

Marijuana has a lot to answer for.

Five dateless students with chin beards sitting in a living room that smells like damp dog, earnestly discussing astral projection while watching *Donnie Darko*.

A jam band from Hove calling themselves The Mary Jane Boys featuring a dreadlocked drummer named Jasper, who went to Harrow, who finish every set segueing 'Midnight Rider' into 'Because I Got High'.

A bewildered-looking teenager stoned out of his gourd in a twenty-four-hour garage, who spent forty-five minutes overwhelmed by the wide array of Cornish pasties on offer, and who ended up panic-buying a bottle of anti-freeze after a few too many concerned looks from the cashier.

Then there's this guy, not content like everybody else to spend his evenings robotically drinking seven cans of cheap extra-strength Polish lager in a row, zoning out in front of *Midsomer Murders* while experiencing mild anxiety about going back to work the next day.

No, he went and put a load of highly potent hydroponic skunk into a Betty Crocker cookie mix and spent the evening staring at a tie-dye tablecloth, unable to feel his legs.

Then the next morning he called in sick to spend the day watching 9/11 conspiracy videos on YouTube, eating cold baked beans straight from the tin, and ignoring letters from the Child Support Agency.

What a picture.

It took a few takes to position it just right, but you've really managed to capture that strange shimmer on the surface of this spinach and chilli stew.

Like the magical rainbow effect on a slice of old ham, it's both beguiling and uncanny.

The glimmering vegetable juice hints at secrets lurking in the depths, unseen mysteries floating around at the periphery of one's vision, sexually ambiguous sprites (or possibly ghouls) working at invisible controls behind the velvet curtain of waking life.

A sloppy green enigma, overcooked to the point of limpness yet bursting with surprises.

It's the perfect image to accompany an online announcement declaring your newfound commitment to a healthy lifestyle.

'Who knew getting in shape could taste so good?!' you lie, on the internet, to people who bullied you at school and family members once merely disinterested but now experiencing deep shame.

Not one 'like'.

Not one word of praise for the murky bowl that represented a graduation from the soggy ninety-second microwave hamburgers of your youth to the vitamin-rich sludge of advanced adulthood.

It's almost as if nobody in the world is paying the slightest bit of attention to you or your sudden adoption of a vegan lifestyle.

You pause to unleash a scream for acknowledgement.

It goes unheard, absorbed by the all-consuming darkness of the abyss and the competing screeches of a thousand chattering skulls.

Then it's back to the kitchen to take some photos o dessert in the vain hope that someone will come in your life and say the words, 'I see you'.

Jemble raises a hand to his head, his fedora feels too tight and he is worried it's cutting off the oxygen to his brain.

He sighs dejectedly.

It was burnt oven chips for dinner tonight, no sauce or seasoning save the bitter salt of his tears.

Once again, Jemble would be a wandering minstrel in the kingdom of the bland.

He pulls out his trusty ukulele and sings a woeful ballad to his dinner.

Lyrically, it concerns a lovely maiden he'd serenaded in the gift shop of the British Museum.

She'd been cruelly snatched from his grasp when a teacher spotted Jemble by the replica figurines of Anubis doffing his hat towards the bemused schoolgirl and promptly frog-marched her away for her own safety.

'Methinks it's time to go to the shops and purchase some comestibles,' Jemble says aloud to an empty room.

The floorboards let out an agonising creak like an old man in pain.

Jemble wonders if the lovely redhead with the lazy eye will be working the tills at the Co-op today.

He means to ask her why she hasn't accepted his friend request on Facebook and to invite her along to his medieval music group's lute tribute to *Monty Python and the Holy Grail*.

Jemble places his plate of chips back in the oven, pulls on a trench coat and leaves the flat with a spring in his step.

This is what happens when a vegan makes their people's version of a sausage.

It's similar to how a child might make mud pies in the back garden following a spell of heavy rain. However, even the most stupid child knows that in reality it is in possession of a handful of earth, not a delicious fudge brownie.

I'm not so sure about vegans. Some of them really do seem taken in by meat simulacra. You begin to wonder if they're naturally credulous, if their future shares a similar trajectory of falling victim to pyramid schemes and bogus officials.

Maybe all it takes to convince these people that what's in front of them is edible is the addition of a small sprig of something green. Look at it, not even parsley. It's a bloody disgrace!

In a certain way it's sweet, perhaps even endearing, that fully grown adults will eat genetically modified soya that's been fashioned into the shape of a cartoon bacon rasher and momentarily imagine they're eating real food.

Maybe they've never let go of childlike innocence, and every mealtime is an exercise of great imagination, a journey into a world of wonder where anything is possible.

Maybe.

Solo roast dinners aren't much fun.

Vegetarian solo roast dinners are even worse.

Two curiously circular splats of nut roast smothered in vegetarian gravy as thick as crude oil.

Frozen carrots, sliced by machine in a factory somewhere in East Anglia to be of uniform shape and size, ever so slightly larger than a one-pound coin or about the same size as a sobriety token from Alcoholics Anonymous, depending on your frame of reference.

The monotony of a low-sodium diet and the sheer tedium of another Sunday spent on your own, being a vegetarian and eating unseasoned potatoes.

If only there was someone who could love you completely, freezer-burnt carrots and all.

Someone with whom you could share the gentle monotony of a Sunday night, who would distract you from the awfulness of the telly, the creeping dread of returning to work for another week, and the ever present awareness at the back of your mind that all existence is finite.

A human being that you could turn to for some momentary solace in a cold, dark, empty universe.

A warm body, a fellow gibbering ape to groom you for ticks and hold your hand when the spiky black claws of reality dig into your soft underbelly.

Someone to share your sickly brown nut roast.

It's almost eleven o'clock and Keith's board game group is nowhere to be seen.

The carefully prepared hors d'oeuvres, stacked like a miniature game of Jenga, are now stone cold.

Keith wonders whether The Guild of Extraordinary Adventurers could still be suffering from the fallout of the great Minotaur sex debacle?

It had been an ugly scene, full of raised voices and accusations of Ogrephobia, as well as a few disparaging remarks about Keith's choice of refreshments.

Keith had found that particularly unfair given he was the only person in the Guild with their own flat in which to host games night and the only person willing to cook. He had noted that several of his fellow adventurers brought their own flasks filled with squash and didn't offer to share with the rest of the group.

The usual suspects, the ones who always had to rush away when the twenty-sided dice needed packing away and there was washing up to be done.

Shortly after sitting down Keith realises that his dungeon master's cape has become trapped under the foot of the sofa.

If he moves suddenly he's in very real danger of asphyxiating himself.

It's no laughing matter; he'd recently seen a wizard nearly decapitate himself in the escalators at Tooting Broadway.

Shit!

There is no way of loosening it.

He'll just have to sit and hope someone turns up to set him free.

The rice paper rolls sit on the plate, disappointing reminders of a lack of motor control and manual dexterity.

It had taken Martin several hours and a fair few botched attempts that went straight in the bin and all he had to show for it was six shitty specimens that looked like goblin cocks clad in Tesco Value condoms. Budget-brand sanitary bin liners stuffed with cat sick. A brace of body bags filled to the brim with a scarecrow's guts.

The analogies are getting more and more tortured and time is running out.

Martin is expecting company for the first time in what seemed like years.

A latecomer to the internet, he'd finally embraced online dating after being assured the World Wide Web wasn't just for *Red Dwarf* fans and paedophiles anymore.

You could also meet what his friend Jemble described as 'female human beings'.

He'd actually managed to meet and go on a date with one. Lunch at Pizza Express, and it hadn't been completely awful. Now it is date number two and he is entertaining at his flat.

Martin is certain his take on Japanese food would win over the heart of Amanda, thirty-seven, likes Prosecco and the novels of Louise Bagshawe; dislikes liars, cheats and people who don't know what they want out of life.

Martin knows exactly what he wants out of life.

Not to be alone. Desperately, painfully, more than anything.

Which is why he's texted her thirty-one times already today to check she is still coming.

Still no response, but there is every chance she has it on silent.

There are those out there who would say it's a bad sign when you can't even be bothered to mix the tuna all the way into the mayonnaise.

They don't know what they're talking about.

You went to all the effort of placing it in a bowl today; that's a definite improvement on eating it straight from the tin while standing over the sink, watching the brine trickle down the plughole and thinking about the last time you were genuinely happy.

The bulk of the food in your kitchen is tinned tuna.

You got into the habit of eating it when you first moved away from home because it always seemed to be on special offer at the supermarket and it brought back memories of packed lunches made by Mother.

Her specially made sandwiches with the crusts lovingly cut off, unwrapped from their clingfilm blankets, were eaten alone under the shade of the old oak tree that acted as a refuge for the less popular children in the playground of your small provincial primary school.

Tuna has been keeping you alive for the last twenty years since you left home.

Unbeknownst to you, its longstanding inclusion in your diet has gifted you with an extraordinary tolerance to the potentially fatal effects of mercury poisoning, although this very same exposure has at times ushered the unwelcome spectre of mad-hatter syndrome through the fragile front door of the paper house that is your mind.

Perhaps if you were aware of the gifts bestowed upon you by this diet of tinned fish you would use these powers for good.

There is no joy to be had in this life.

We're all alone in a kitchen of cruelty, overwhelmed by the acrid fumes of our incinerated dinners.

There is no escape from the inevitability of our demise.

Eventually everything burns down around you, leaving you clutching miserably on to a hockey puck of a pizza as dark as the bags beneath your bloodshot eyes.

What kind of creator would fashion a world so cruel?

A world where a thing so beautiful in its simplicity as cheese and tomato on bread can turn into a pizza shit.

A world where someone would break up with you because all you ever wanted to do was smoke weed, play politically dubious video games and eat pizza.

A world where a momentary indiscretion like spending two hours obsessively stalking through your ex's Facebook photos and worrying about all her new, attractive and motivated-looking friends can lead you to forget the frozen pizza in your oven.

It's a cruel, uncaring world.

So much so that it's caused you to start reading Nietzsche, wear turtlenecks and develop an interest in old black-and-white photographs.

Your boy Friedrich would have had something to say about pizza. Probably along the lines of that without it life would be a mistake.

He'd have understood you and the heroic struggle you were involved in.

It's a shame he had to be so dead.

That big stupid meaty grin isn't fooling anyone.

This fondness you have for manipulating pork products into grotesque parodies of human emotion betrays the emotional disconnect you experience every day of your life.

Feelings, remember them?

It's been a while since you experienced them bubbling away under the surface.

Apart from the all-consuming rage you feel when someone slights you, that is. Followed by the brief glimmer of satisfaction you feel when you righteously smite said transgressor.

Generally, it's been a steady cruise on shallow waters. There are no great waves of sensation to rock the steady ship you've been sailing on.

The smile you wear at work and with family is as artificial as the one you've contrived with roughly cut sausages.

Roughly cut sausages that sit atop a thin batter pancake forming a friendly face not unlike the mask of sanity you've been wearing ever since you became a manager in telesales.

The subject line in every email you receive seems to be the same: 'FEED ME A CAT'.

The recent habit you've developed of sleeping overnight in the stationery cupboard so you can observe your colleagues undetected first thing in the morning.

You're learning a lot about human behaviour, about the weaknesses of the people in your office. Like the fact that Mike is allergic to peanuts, that Rachel doesn't like spiders and how Alan is absolutely terrified of you.

All useful information; something to ponder while having breakfast.

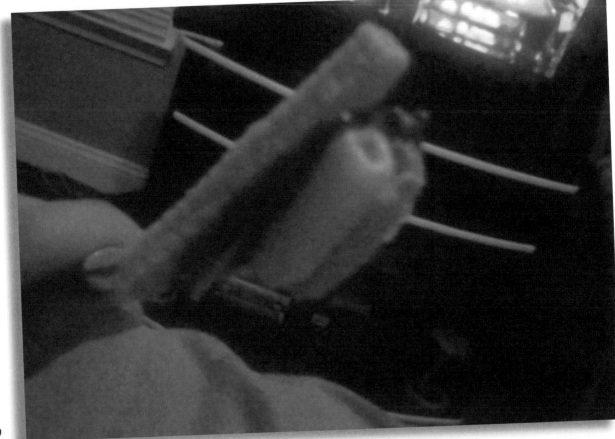

For the longest time, Saturdays meant sitting around in your pants and watching the *Come Dine With Me* marathon.

Often you'd indulge the daydream of applying for the show and winning everyone over with your extrovert personality and stylish take on modern British cuisine.

Sadly, it's evident from the fact that you often go several days at a time without leaving your flat that you're not really an extrovert.

Talking loudly to yourself, singing along to the radio and doing that offensively bad German accent while washing up ('ve haf ways of making you do ze dishes') doesn't mean you have a larger-than-life personality.

No, it's a sign that you've been steeping in the stagnant waters of your loneliness for so long now that you've finally turned.

Like a load of laundry sitting in the machine for too long, which you wear to the shops anyway because it's that or go naked.

The thought of being part of a group of strangers sharing food, laughter and possibly romance over the course of a week fills your heart with a painful longing.

'Fuck it!' you say out loud in the Al Pacino voice you've started doing again after *Scent of a Woman* was on the telly a few nights ago. 'I'm going to be on their goddamn cookery show and ain't no needledick producer going to tell me otherwise. Al Pacino.'

You still haven't broken out of your habit of ending all your impressions with the name of the person you're mimicking.

One of the many reasons why you don't get asked to places where there are other people.

Brenda is making an apple pie like the kind her grandmother used to bake: shapeless, soggy and prone to falling apart at any moment.

It occurs to Brenda that the old woman who had haunted her childhood with undermining behaviour and bad baking would have used those very same adjectives to describe the endless source of disappointment that was her granddaughter.

In what police would describe as a 'freak occurrence', when Brenda was but a tiny baby her mother and father had been carried away from Brighton's Palace Pier by a flock of deranged gulls.

And so she was left to be raised by Grandmother Murray (never a 'gran' or a 'nana'), a stick-thin woman with a natty moustache who liked to pinch her ever-so-slightly chubby granddaughter around the waist and call her a miniature sumo.

She'd write disparaging remarks about Brenda's weight and pimply complexion on small pieces of paper and bake them into biscuits for the little girl to find.

Grandmother Murray called these her 'misfortune cookies'.

She'd hand them out to the other children at Brenda's school, encouraging them to collect the scrawled insults within as if they were Pokémons or Pogs, or whatever young people are collecting at any given time.

The man at the supermarket who had sold Brenda the ingredients for her pie still had some saved in the coin purse of his Spiderman wallet.

He'd shown Brenda as she'd paid for her shopping. Brenda regarded them with some envy, as they were, in fact, quite rare.

'The greatest trick the devil ever played on the world was low-fat crisps.'

So said the trendy pastor with the footballer's haircut and the cheeky grin as he passed around the bowl of cheesy puffs.

You weren't a religious person at all but for the last three weeks you'd been attending an Alpha course at the nearby evangelical church.

There were always drinks and snacks available afterwards and there was even an occasional weekend barbecue.

It was simple: feign an interest in God in exchange for free food or carry on stealing your housemate's tinned sardines and horrible 'healthy' crisps.

Figuring that as long as they thought your soul was still up for grabs and not exclusively devoted to Princess Leia, the Christians would be nice to you and keep on fattening you up with cake and crisps, twenty-first-century Croydon's answer to the loaves and fishes, you kept on going despite not believing a word that was being said.

The alternative to spending more time with your housemate was actually less appealing than lying to a group of trusting strangers.

They were all very smiley and even though none of it made much sense and there was the occasional moment of crippling guilt you had to admit that you were a lot less lonely nowadays.

There might even have been a bit of interest from a couple of the single Christians; you'd been getting a *lot* of smiles.

Clearly it was far less hassle to go with the flow and just get baptised.

What sound does a human soul make as it escapes the body?

Does it hiss like a newly opened bottle of fizzy drink?

Maybe it squeaks like the wheels of the shopping trolley pushed by the homeless man near your flat, the sight of whom always fills you with guilt for having just spent nine pounds on a bottle of wine.

Perhaps it makes a sad defeated sigh, like the noise your dad made when you told him that next term at university you'd be taking a gender theory module rather than the one on business German that you'd previously discussed.

Or possibly it's a little sob, similar to the sound you made later on when you decided to drop out of that course altogether because you had literally no idea what anyone was talking about.

Surely it has to be the sound you hear after sitting down to eat a bowl of waffle crisps and fizzy guacamole so old that it has sprouted a mane of cress?

You don't want to keep eating because you can feel it making you ill, but you're so hungry, you can't stop.

The cacophony of explosive vomiting, a violent conversation with God on the porcelain telephone, a Technicolor yawn into the abyss... that's the sound your soul makes as it leaves the body.

A lifetime of misunderstanding the idiom 'to get your oats' meant that Barry was often perceived as being inappropriate at work when in fact all he wanted was to talk about his breakfast.

Barry struggled with social situations almost as much as he struggled to get a consistent blend to his porridge.

It didn't help that he insisted on sticking massive chunks of apple into it before he'd had a chance to give it a proper stir.

He was another victim of the kind of television advertising that repeatedly depicted people enjoying 'healthy cereals' with lashings of perfectly ripe fresh fruit.

All Barry wanted was some Ricicles and a hug from a human woman.

No one really wants to eat shit like porridge or muesli, and if they did they'd have it heaped with sugar or syrup, not out-of-season fruit.

The average cereal eater would prefer to have five bowls of Crunchy Nut Cornflakes and then a Mars bar and then a Marlboro Light – and then fall into a diabetic coma in front of Jeremy Kyle.

Soon they'd fall into familiar sugar-fuelled nightmares of being trapped in a cereal café somewhere in deepest Shoreditch, surrounded by a bunch of kidults clad in animal onesies and limited-edition New Balance, eager to burn them within a gigantic wicker Honey Monster as an offering to the cereal gods.

The hotdogs had slipped out of the can still stuck together in a crude pyramid formation.

They looked into Gareth's eyes like a small pile of logs that might sit next to a cabin out in the woods.

Not the woods near him, though.

Those were all full of conference-league footballers sitting in their cars enjoying a cheeky Nando's with a spot of dogging and a few unemployed migrants forced to live off the land, unable to afford the plane fare back home, the promise of a Great Britain having turned out to be a damp squib.

No, Gareth had in mind a rather more romantic vision of the great American wilderness. An arboreal paradise fit to raise an Abraham Lincoln or a Grizzly Adams. Fitting, as the hotdogs were in fact labelled as being 'Classic American style' – full of pig's lips and anuses.

As was customary after a long day at the office, Gareth sat with his beans and his pyramid of pork in the perpetually darkened communal kitchen he and his three housemates share.

Clad in flannel and with a healthy beard he was very much a lumbersexual.

The only thing separating him from a classic woodsman was the fact he'd spent a lot of time and money cultivating this look – and that because as a junior administrator he was not required to swing an axe, his hands were soft and uncalloused as a newborn babe.

Have you seen this pie?

It was last seen in a slightly overweight single man's flat on a Saturday, roughly around the time that *Doctor Who*'s on.

It's thought to contain hormone-rich South American beef and answers to the name 'Fray'.

Police are concerned the pie may have met the unidentified male on the internet as part of an online shop.

They are asking the public to look closely at the picture: a slice of silent misery, fresh out of the tin, preserved for posterity in a small and slightly blurred photo reminiscent of one of those CCTV stills shown on the evening news capturing the last moment the member of a stag party was last seen alive before he was found a few days later, floating in a nearby canal wreathed in old Sainsbury's bags and discarded contraceptives. Pure pastry-covered tragedy.

Please report to the police if you see anything suspicious.

As R. Kelly told many young women over the years, 'Age ain't nothing but a number'.

You tell yourself the same thing as you find yourself well into your fifth decade, a typical evening's meal consisting of Welsh rarebit and Monster Munch.

It may only be glorified cheese on toast and children's crisps that's on the menu tonight in the flat of perpetual bachelorhood, but you still like to think of yourself as being that little bit more hip and that little bit cooler than the sad old blokes you went to school with.

They all gave up on fashion years ago, but you refuse to acquiesce to the onslaught of middle age by buying your jeans from the same place as you do your weekly shop. You still have standards you tell yourself, as you chew on a stale pickled-onion crisp.

It's the same with pop music: you're not ready to give up on it without a serious fight. As long as there are taste-making music blogs around, which are reasonably reliable and don't feature too much free jazz and atonal industrial noise, you're still willing to pretend that your most listened to album of all time isn't Queen's *Greatest Hits II*.

Most of your old mates would seriously struggle to compile a credible Best Albums of the Year list; you could name ten must-listen-to albums off the top of your head that would blow their dad-rock shit out of the water.

I mean, so what if they've all got families now, right?

Sod them if they're too busy to come to Glastonbury with you again this year.

Pancake Day comes but once a year, and just like your ageing alcoholic father's birthday you generally forget about it until two days after the fact.

Unlike Dad, however, pancakes won't hold it against you and ring you up at four in the morning to drunkenly make their annual threat of disinheriting you in favour of Cats Protection.

Pancakes would never do that.

They won't make promises to drive you to Blackpool to watch the Illuminations then decide to drink a bottle of cooking sherry and piss themselves instead.

Nope, they're basically just flour and water, which means they have far less capacity to disappoint you than the seed carrier who shares half the responsibility for bringing you into this miserable world.

This year you're having a go at doing Pancake Day properly.

You wandered down to the supermarket and bought all the ingredients specially.

Perhaps this somewhat missed the intended purpose of the pre-Lenten feast but then again, what do chocolate eggs and a day off work watching James Bond movies really have to do with the resurrection of Christ?

What's this? Shit! Pancakes, they're not actually that easy, are they? You can almost hear Dad's boozed-up mocking laughter.

Oh, cruel life!

Hang on – you can *definitely* hear your dad now.

He's outside in the garden arguing with your neighbour. He's got his sports jacket on backwards and he's covered in piss.

The problem with uploading every meal you eat onto social media is that no matter how many sickly filters you whack on top of your photos you cannot disguise the fact that sometimes what you're recording for posterity is simply an egg on top of some broken bread.

Egg that's not so much been scrambled as had the shit kicked out of it in the pub car park.

Those filters, though. Someone needs to say something.

You might think that the sepia tint you apply to every picture on your phone makes everything look retro in a good way, like it's from an existential seventies movie that takes place in the desert and features a lot of people who look bored staring at ceiling fans.

But it doesn't.

It makes everything look brown.

Your yellow eggs, brown.

Your blue plate, brown.

Your brown bread, even more brown.

Every photo unbearably brown.

People are starting to wonder if you've got some manner of neurological impairment, that you can't fully perceive anything until it's been put through a process of brownisation.

You won't stop, though.

They'll have to prise your smartphone from your cold, dead hands.

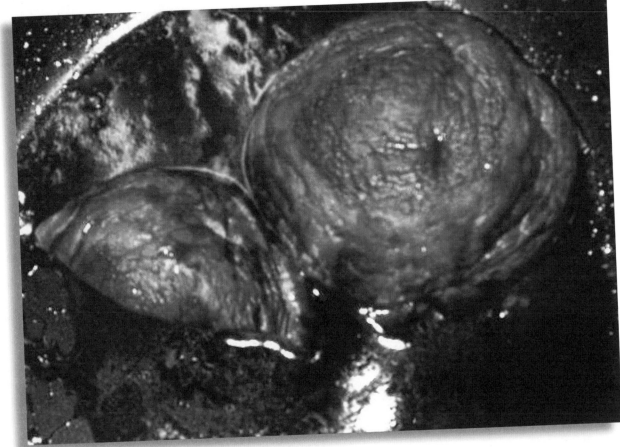

Warren watches the mushrooms frying side by side.

Shrivelled, leaking juice, not smelling particularly great.

They were like the elderly couple he'd sat behind on the bus earlier that day.

Warren's heart grows heavy when he realises that he may never be as close to another human being as the mushroom that now clings to its fungal life partner in a desperate embrace.

He looks at all the dirty mushroom juice filling his frying pan. They had looked so plump in the packet.

He wonders if he's doing it all wrong.

Where was all this liquid coming from?

'Who would have thought the old man had so much juice in him?'

Warren is talking aloud to himself.

No sooner has he finished speaking than there's a tremendous racket from above.

Warren's upstairs neighbour doesn't like the sound of Warren's voice and punctuates his lonely soliloquies by loudly banging on her floor and passively calling him a wanker, as in 'That wanker's talking to himself again' or 'Why won't that downstairs wanker just shut up? Shut up!'

Looking down at the soggy mushrooms Warren realises that he has been crying into his cooking.

Could he alone possibly have been the source of all the unwanted moistness?

Warren reasons that his near-constant sobbing could well be keeping his weight down.

He throws the mushrooms in the bin and goes out for a kebab.

Like a half-arsed Wile E. Coyote laying a trap for the Road Runner, Paul concealed his vegan sausages under a generous portion of birdseed.

He had ventured too far down this highway to turn back.

For weeks and weeks he had talked incessantly of his commitment to a more ethical lifestyle and his renunciation of all things animal based.

Loudly, and within earshot of the whole company, he'd only been trying to impress the attractive new temp, who'd casually mentioned that her Doc Martens were of the vegan variety. She had seemed only politely interested, soon accepting a full-time job at a petrochemicals company, a few hundred miles away in Swindon.

Now Paul has to live with the consequences of his big mouth.

It was like the martial-arts classes all over again. The sheer hell of running around a cold scout hut with a group of men deemed psychologically unsuitable for the Territorial Army.

If only he'd shut up about it and not made a big deal of getting all the veggie cookbooks and sacks of supplemental grains delivered to reception at work he could be having a fucking steak right now.

Instead he'd chucked away all the food in his flat that came with a face and was stuck with cupboards full of grains and pulses he couldn't even pronounce.

Why would he never learn?

Before you rush off to leave a scathing review of this book on that internationally renowned website that started off selling books and now specialises in harvesting the tears, souls and firstborn children of their employees I can assure you there is no product placement in this book.

It's not for want of trying, though.

You would think given the number of times the armpit-flavoured polystyrene atrocities they masquerade to the world as crisps appeared in this slim volume, Monster Munch might have kicked a few quid in my direction.

Strangely enough they didn't want any part of it. Neither did SPAM.

They told me they were trying to move away from the 'sad bastards and overgrown children' demographic with which they had been historically associated.

With Monster Munch the plan was to phase out the monster part of the brand and replace it with something more appealing to the eighteen to thirty age range.

Like affordable housing or sexting.

I regretted sending so many emails in which I used phrases such as 'corporate synergy' and 'cross-platform promotion'.

I'd been all too willing to prostitute myself to the crisp companies and merchants of processed pork.

They could clearly smell the desperation burning through the screen as they read the litany of lies in which I earnestly expressed my desire to become a brand ambassador.

In fact, the only company who had any interest in working with me was Dignitas.

Turned out they were very keen to get in touch with my contributors.

I was a teenager in the mid-nineties, just as the internet made its way into the classroom.

In those days it was a rite of passage to visit the most horrific sites you could imagine, download an image of a mangled corpse or two randy granddads getting intimate with one another, using the school's painfully slow dial-up and then set the sordid pictures as the desktop background for the person sitting next to you.

As harrowing as some of those images were, none could prepare me for the horrors I'd encounter in the world of food blogging.

If that sounds like hyperbole consider this: if you see terrifying photographs of a naked old man engaged in mind-boggling carnal acts what exactly is that going to put you off?

Working in a retirement home?

Volunteering for meals on wheels?

For most jaded young people those options aren't even on the table to begin with.

Bad pictures of food, though. Look at too many of those and you're liable to develop an eating disorder.

Day after day I spend scrutinising prolapsed loaves of egg-filled bread, meat smears and oddly sexual plates of malformed sausage.

Every bite of food I take is ash in my mouth, my mind an unceasing sideshow of desolate images.

I live off grain alcohol and plain white rolls, the pleasures of food now forever denied to me.

This is my penance for having lived a trite and meaningless existence.

And for all the hundreds of naked grandfathers hidde throughout my friend Ben's GCSE coursework...

Sorry.

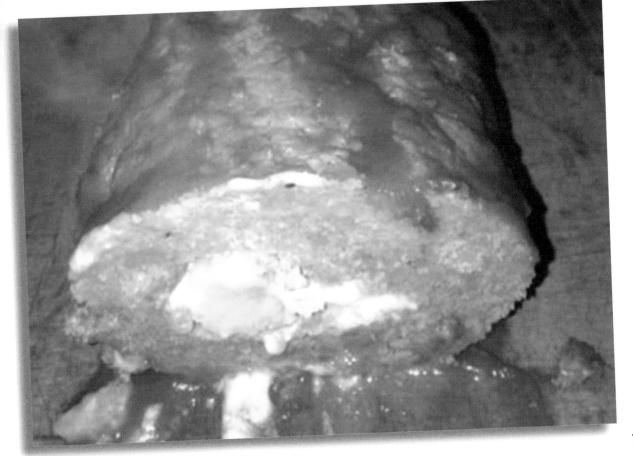

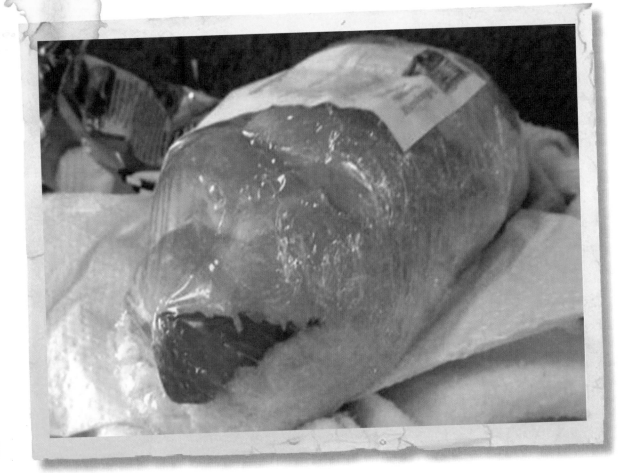

'Janet, come quick, look here, look at this sandwich. Doesn't it... it's... it's just like a dolphin, isn't it?'

'Oh my goodness, yes! Yes, it is! Michael, we simply have to buy this for Maxwell. He absolutely adores dolphins.'

Maxwell sits in an aqua blue room, the walls covered in images of marine life.

Somewhere from within those walls comes the piped-in screeching of a bottlenose dolphin.

He cannot locate the source, although he has tried several times to burrow into the plasterwork and cease the infernal chatter of the hated marine mammal.

Maxwell could not even escape the squeaky dead-eyed non-fish at mealtimes. Sitting in an adult-sized high chair, spoon-fed by Janet, her own abnormally large proboscis making her look uncannily like a dolphin in a henna wig.

And now this.

This roll.

The final indignity.

Maxwell would take it no more.

At night he plotted. Soon he would break free from this porpoise penitentiary, burn it down and reclaim what was left of his old life.

Then he would drive to the nearest reasonably sized aquarium, climb into a tank and punch the first dolphin that swam up to him right in its smug face.

Green vegetables haven't touched your lips in years. To be fair, human lips haven't touched your lips in years either.

Human affection is something you must take wherever you can find it.

Hence those overlong hugs you give your best friend whenever you see him, clinging on just that little too tightly.

You might get away with it if you rationed the cloying embraces to one per social engagement, but you insist on a cuddle every time he comes back from the kitchen with a fresh beer.

It's no coincidence that the people you know are taking longer and longer to respond to your emails and text messages.

Never mind, you've always got chicken nuggets to fill that aching, desperate void in your soul. Mountains and mountains of comforting chunks of bite-size processed chicken.

Processed chicken that won't ever tell you 'I'm sorry, mate, but I'm battling a chest infection and can't go to the pub', and then proceed to post pictures of their night out at the local Wetherspoons on Facebook for the whole world to see.

Chicken nuggets don't consciously decide to stop returning your calls and then move halfway across the country without telling you.

They're all the friends you need, and they don't get weird if you try and sleep with them.

Life, it's basically a sitcom with no laughter track that continues far past the point at which it ceased to be funny.

You stick with it because it's familiar and always on, but you know exactly where it's going, even the occasional killing off of a minor character here and there fails to stir much interest in you.

Still, the thought of its inevitable cancellation occupies your thoughts in the twilight hours, filling your heart with unknown despair.

Tinned meals, so compact, so straightforward.

They line up so neatly on the cupboard shelf, each one representing a unit of time you will spend engaged in the act of eating.

There is an order, a sense of structure, in seeing your future meals all present and accounted for sitting adjacent to one another in identical-sized containers. It doesn't matter that it tastes horrible: it exists, that's enough.

Each one is a meal lasting roughly twenty-two minutes.

Long enough for an episode of that sitcom you hate but always end up watching.

Perhaps it will be one of the older ones, you hope. One of the ones from when it used to be good.

It never is, though.

Despite what the professional bantersauruses that once presented *Top Gear* might say, Mexico is a proud country with a rich culinary tradition.

They were just trying to generate cheap heat for a once-noble show that used to be about tedious car reviews rather than old men in the grips of crises having racist japes and advocating for big petroleum.

Mexican food isn't like vomit – Mexican food is delicious.

Have you ever eaten a chimichanga? They're amazing.

Don't listen to Richard Hammond, the man wears driving gloves and lives off Ginsters pasties and KitKats, and whatever else he can forage at the twenty-four-hour garage.

It's worth bearing in mind that even during years of horrific violence perpetrated by the drug cartels, nothing that occurred in Mexico was even remotely as heinous as Jeremy Clarkson in a tight pair of jeans, pulling a face and doing a banter.

Let's look at the photographic evidence.

The person responsible for this taco atrocity ('tacocity') is clearly English.

English people really don't get Mexican food. They pronounce fajitas 'fadge-itters' and eat at Chiquito. They relocate to sunny paradises and complain that they can't get an adequately artery-clogging breakfast despite an abundance of delicious local produce.

They can't be trusted.

I refer you back to the photo.

Look.

Those are Sugar Puffs in there.

I swear it.

The lonely chef responsible for this culinary hodgepodge is an example of what's known as a 'fragment eater'.

Worried about running out of food they'll never finish anything completely. Their fridges are constantly full of half-empty tins of beans, gnawed-on hunks of cheese, crudely torn strips of sliced ham.

Towards the end of the month, when the money's running out, the fragment eater employs a technique known as 'scraping the back of the fridge'.

Everything that looks vaguely edible is thrown together; the final third of a jar of curry sauce, a handful of microwaveable rice, fragments of luncheon meat, all mixed up and sitting side by side on the same plate.

This scattershot approach to dining is indicative of a deeper inability to complete things.

Screenplays, charity bike rides, sexual encounters... these are all things that tend to fizzle out for the fragment eater shortly after they've been undertaken.

At work you'll often see them wandering around with a clipboard in hand, a vaguely purposeful aspect to their walk disguising the fact they no longer have a clue as to what they're doing.

No one ever asks them what they're doing either because, like their approximation of a meal, it sort of looks like something's going on.

Better not to ask.

Let them get on with it.

Good luck with all that!

People who care about things are the worst.

The woman at work who asked you to sponsor her desert bike ride in aid of veterans of a war you'd have probably disagreed with if you gave a shit.

The drone from Human Resources who informed you that if you were going to make your Facebook profile public you couldn't list your title at work as 'submissive bottom'.

The housemate who repeatedly asks you to clean up the microwave covered in six-day-old pasta sauce, tearfully knocking on the door and telling you, 'It'll attract mice!'

People with genuine pride in their work, people who believe in things, people who sign petitions and go on demonstrations.

Who are they?

What's wrong with them?

Why do they always want other people to care about things too?

The last ethical decision you made was choosing not to eat a turkey dinosaur because it looked sad.

Not a single solitary fuck did you give about the caged bird and how it sings or pecks itself bald out of sheer hopeless desperation.

The breadcrumb-covered T-Rex had simply made you feel strangely wistful, a sensation not dissimilar to the slight tingling in the balls you felt after using a tea-tree shower gel.

That had been overwhelming.

Now it was time to return to what you did best: standing with an ear cupped to the bedroom wall, listening to the muted sobs of your housemate.

181

Look, someone's disgusting feet made it into the book.

This was a conscious decision on my part to try and appeal to that certain demographic of people who are into weird podiatric shit.

You know the sort – men of a certain age who spend a lot of time alone in their sheds, develop disturbing fixations with local newsreaders and spend a lot of time getting blocked on Twitter too.

Obviously it's very difficult to take a picture of your dinner without exposing some part of your anatomy to the world.

In fact, most of the leaked celebrity photographs from way back when started off harmlessly enough as a quick shot of some lasagna before escalating into the full-frontal nudity you now see.

It speaks volumes that none of the so-called journalists who recently wrote salacious articles about the terrible breach of privacy mentioned anything about Jennifer Lawrence's fabulous Shepherd's Pie.

So much for ethics in food journalism.

Exposed toes aside, this is a rather jolly-looking meal.

A presumed human, probably some bloody student, has deprived a duck somewhere of a lovely stale baguette for the purposes of dunking it into some queasily orange tomato soup.

Why is the spoon standing up on its own?

How thick is this soup?

Has the cook noticed?

Do they even care?

They're clearly too preoccupied with making sure that their feet are on point to care about the hot saucepan full of sludge that's slowly beginning to catch fire on the hob.

It took a while, but you finally managed to move out of your parents' house.

Congratulations! Now all that previously disposable income you enjoyed spending on *Doctor Who* merchandise will be sunk into paying the rent for a poorly ventilated shoebox.

At least now you're in charge at dinnertime.

No more complaining to your mum that all the fried food she's cooking is aggravating your acne. There's a new sheriff in town and his name ain't Reggie Hammond.

It's Keith, and if Keith wants to slam back a couple of multivitamins and fill a mixing bowl up with cookie crisp cereal nobody's going to stop him.

Cereal for supper; the first few times you do it feels a little knowing, like perhaps you're sending up the whole idea of being a thirty-year-old man who struggles even with entry-level pasta dishes.

You try and convince yourself you're being tongue-in-cheek about it, that eventually you'll buy a wok and get into South East Asian cuisine, maybe even do that induction session at the gym you've been putting off for so long, and try to meet someone.

Nah, that's not going to happen, is it?

Be honest.

There are still a shitload of those little plastic dinosaurs that they're giving away with every packet you've yet to collect.

Neon green velociraptor, big blue triceratops, historically inaccurate cavemen of various different hues.

Adulthood can wait.

It's a pivotal moment in your development as a desperate man-child; there's no need to rush anything.

Funnily enough, a diet that's heavily reliant on Iceland's frozen party selection and ketchup isn't necessarily going to give you the essential trace elements and nutrients your body needs to live.

Hence the zinc tablets.

If you're in need of those it means you're not quite getting something from your diet, something important that prevents you getting a cold every fortnight, something that will stop the skin from falling off your perpetually chafed face.

Zinc is known for having a restorative effect on the male libido. That's why alongside hand lotion and baby wipes it's an essential part of any home onanist's emergency self-abuse kit.

Thank God for robots taking over all the jobs at the supermarket. They don't judge you for shameful lifestyle choices.

If only they'd let you scan your own booze you'd never have to talk to another human being as long as you lived.

A weakness for meals consisting entirely of frozen party snacks means that precious zinc is keeping your intimate bits in working order while the rest of your body is slowly engulfed by saturated fats.

Eventually you'll have to lift up several bellies before you can interfere with yourself, but zinc will keep you tumescent long after the wontons have left the rest of your body a desolate and flabby wasteland.

Steve grew up in a family that didn't have much time for people with pretensions and fancy ways.

He'd never live down his mother's uncomprehending rage upon being offered a sun-dried tomato in the local supermarket.

Nor could he forget his father's suspicion of a new neighbour who subscribed to the *Guardian* and once used the word 'sesquipedalian' in a conversation about the council's annual letter detailing the Christmas bin-collection schedule.

They would have been mortified to see Steve eating off square plates, *black* ones no less, and going on about pulled pork to anyone who'd listen.

There was seemingly no end to Steve's metropolitan affectations these days.

He was even leaving bits of skin on his potatoes when he made mash.

Mum and Dad would shake their heads if they saw that.

'That's not rustic, Steven, it's plain lazy is what it is.'

He could hear their nagging voices in his head.

They were asking him why he'd not met a nice girl yet and settled down.

They were loudly wondering why he'd put up a poster for the Green Party in the window of his front room.

They were telling him again and again that he didn't even like pulled pork, that he was just trying to be cool, that waiting for him in the freezer were the potato waffles he truly desired.

Caroline didn't used to like tuna.

The strong metallic flavours and ever-present possibility that she was in fact eating the dead flesh of a smiling bottlenose dolphin put her off consuming the popular sandwich filler/fish.

It didn't help that the lingering smell of brine in which the chunks of deep-sea fish were suspended brought back unpleasant memories of having to walk past the men's toilets at work during that awful summer when the air conditioning broke down and the cleaners went on strike.

Caroline had only really started eating it so that she could make herself that little bit more desirable to the neighbourhood cats. Cats whose company she craved on the long lonely nights when her most recent attempt at dieting forced her to say goodbye to her old friends Ben and Jerry.

She had taken to keeping a small handful of fish flakes in her coat as she found it attracted the normally aloof ginger tom she'd named Damian

Lewis, after the other attractive redhead who featured prominently in her rich interior life.

Caroline's cat luring had unforeseen consequences.

One evening after she temporarily passed out on the kitchen floor, having accidentally sliced her finger off with a jagged lid, Caroline awoke to find the cat eating the mangled, bloodied stump.

Caroline was barely able to fend off the surprisingly muscular animal driven mad by the overwhelming stench of fish in the flat.

She was forced to bludgeon Damian Lewis to death with the half-opened tin.

Her tears that night were pure brine.

This plate of meatballs and gloop comes to us from Sweden, a land of social democracy and flaxen-haired melancholists.

Statistics seem to suggest that the perception of the Swedes as being a people driven to suicidal despair by Ingmar Bergman and Abba is erroneous.

My own personal experience of the tendency towards bleak introspection in Swedes is shaped by a gift I received for my twelfth birthday from a close family friend in Stockholm.

A thoughtful and generous gift, but perhaps a book of poetry by Ted Hughes exploring his feelings of grief and despair following the death of his mother is not the best present for a child who frequently wet the bed well into his teens.

Call me crazy, but I also wouldn't suggest *Scenes from a Marriage* for a lads' night in.

Whether it's your parents' mortality or the gradual decay of a marriage, there's something in Sweden to depress everyone.

The dinner that you bought in IKEA and ate alone after spending all day arguing with your dad over the size of the bookshelves that were for your much smaller new flat.

You knew the Billy bookcase was far too big for the car.

It was wishful thinking.

So too was adding all the juice from your frozen meatballs to your mashed potato castle.

Now everything is sodden and sludgy, like the inevitable disappointment of melting snow as it turns to brown slush.

By now you've probably decided whether or not you enjoy the repetitious nature of seeing poorly composed pictures of average to poor food accompanied by what people who are not fans of mine have described as 'shit, unfunny and increasingly laboured captions'.

Perhaps you're confined to bed, riddled with disease and sticking to the sheets and this is your only reading material.

Maybe you're on a train, using your Kindle to flick between this and dinosaur erotica while telling everyone at work you're reading *Anna Karenina* for the third time.

Whether you like it or not, at this stage you may well be saying to yourself, 'Hold on a minute, is that the same big blue tray from earlier? What the hell is going on here?'

I'm telling it to you straight: it's not the same tray.

Who would believe that two single men in their thirties living hundreds of miles away were independently drawn to the same institutional-looking trays in sad sack blue?

Somewhere out there in China there's a great big factory exclusively making these big blue bastards for all the prisons, hospitals, oil rigs and poor lonely sods across the length and breadth of the British Isles.

They can be found for sale only in the very darkest recesses of small-town 99p stores.

The same place, perhaps, that you can get hold of Family Circle brand biscuits, Family Circle being one of Dante's lesser-known circles of hell.

It's Saturday night and Cliff is completely free and single, relatively young, and in possession of two thirds of a full head of hair.

The world is full of possibilities, so, as is tradition on the weekend, he is at home spending the evening sitting naked in front of a laptop with a big bowl of leftover pulses and an overripe avocado...

Playing computer games. Cliff's more primal urges had been thoroughly dampened by the chemical cosh of antidepressants.

Tonight's game was 'Suspicious Googling', wherein the goal was to search the internet with a string of queries that by themselves might not appear particularly unusual but when taken together form a worrying trend. Fertiliser, Bicarbonate of soda, Tower Bridge, Shane Richie...

The primary objective was to arouse the suspicion of all the major collectors of personal data like MI5, GCHQ, Facebook, and a certain well-known supermarket chain and the legion of indentured child servants they force to work for them in appalling conditions tallying up the reward points for their loyalty cards.

You thought it was all done with algorithms and robots?

No, it was always child slaves.

Why, you might ask, would anyone want to appear on a watch list for one of those terrifying organisations?

Well, why do people grow moustaches and get into burlesque or become vegans or homeschool their children?

Because human beings desperately crave recognition and attention.

Even if it's overwhelmingly negative.

Even if it means having your front door kicked in and a black bag forced over your head.

Everyone wants to be recognised.

Franklin hadn't been welcome at his family's annual Easter celebrations since the year he'd got completely smashed on dark rum, turned up at his parents' house dressed as a bunny and proceeded to punch his brother-in-law and call his niece and nephew 'grasping little shits'.

It didn't bother him all that much; he was never one for roast lamb and the suffocating love of a close-knit family.

He never did particularly well in the egg hunt and no one else shared his enthusiasm for getting drunk and speculating about which public figures might be secret paedophiles.

Home alone and Franklin could enjoy three different starches in one meal, something his mother would never have allowed.

Cooking was no bother, either; the local Turkish-owned grill house around the corner was more than happy to deliver straight to his flat. They didn't care one jot if it was Easter Sunday or not and for the reasonable sum of fifty pence they'd even boil and peel an egg as a little extra for the megabox for one.

When the delivery came he was often able to grab a few precious seconds of conversation and even the odd moment of real human contact when he placed his five pounds fifty into the hands of the delivery boy.

Never could Franklin have suspected as a child that one day he'd have a closer relationship with the chap from Carlos Kebabs than with his own father.

Still, he reflected as he stuffed a handful of cold chips into his mouth, he'd always been the black sheep of the family.

Is there any better place to enjoy a boiled egg, carrot and spaghetti surprise than on a piss-soaked mattress during the hottest summer in British history?

On the rare occasions you have company, you go to great lengths to explain that it's not your piss that's left a massive stain in the shape of Donald Duck right in the middle of the bedding that also doubles as your sofa and dining table.

'No,' you say with a smile, 'don't worry, the piss came with the place' – forgetting, of course, that night a few weeks after you'd moved in when you did indeed christen the linen with a few pints of recycled beer.

Hot July nights and there's an ungodly funk that's emanating from your studio flat.

The windows are all painted shut and you're living off boiled eggs.

The fear that every time you step out you're bringing the smell of your sulfurous domicile with you is tangible.

To compensate, you've been drenching yourself in Lynx deodorant and now you smell like a junior estate agent who's inadvertently asphyxiated himself getting ready for a night on the razz.

You're far too warm and sweaty at night, partly because no one ever taught you about the differences between polyester and cotton let alone thread counts, whatever the hell those are.

The mini fridge overflows with carrots, eggs and globs of mayonnaise.

It's unclear why you only seem to have these items in the flat at any one time; you vaguely remember reading about how you could live indefinitely off the three foodstuffs in a time of crisis.

This is a crisis, isn't it?

It may look like a plate of cat sick in which persons unknown have artfully hidden a few cherry tomatoes, but this is in fact an omelette.

Omelettes seem to be one of those dishes people who can cook assume are an easy gateway dish for those who live in mortal fear of any method more complex than three minutes in the microwave, stir, return to microwave for three minutes.

They're not, though: they're incredibly difficult and deeply unrewarding.

Omelettes are the very epitome of the joyless and technical dishes my old food technology teacher took great delight in seeing me fail at miserably, with my inability to keep the shell from getting into the yolk and my dyspraxic attempts at flipping the egg mess.

Yes, while cooking your omelette, you have to flip it about five times a minute because otherwise it goes black on one side and stays raw on the other.

If, like me, you have a great deal of difficulty tying your shoelaces or safely getting out of bed in the morning, you're liable to end up with a heavy heap of prolapsed protein much like that in the accompanying picture.

Haven't we evolved beyond stealing eggs from birds?

When men in wax jackets pilfer the unborn offspring of kestrels and eagles they're rightly denounced as weirdos, so why do we turn a blind eye when it's happening to chickens?

It's classism, pure and simple.

So stop with the eggs, stop with the horrible, horrible omelettes.

For a brief period of time a man named Kev shared with me some of the most personal snapshots of his booze and bottled-sauce sodden life.

These pictures weren't of childhood friends or of family holidays taken as a boy. Nor were they close-ups of his genitals in various states of arousal.

However, thankful as I am that I've never been sexted by a middle-aged man, the images I received were arguably as intimate as those of his todger might have been.

These were stark images from the fringe of our society, an insight into the life of one of this dismal island's forgotten people; a winter postcard from a derelict seaside town where the pier has been burned down by yobs, the fish and chips are seasoned with piss and tears, and where the seagulls circle the old and infirm, waiting for their chance to strike.

This was Kev's life story told to me through a series of badly composed photographs of his dinner.

A sausage sandwich enjoyed straight from the chopping board eaten in front of the computer, no need for bourgeois niceties like plates or cutlery.

The weathered cuff of an old sweatshirt an adequate substitute for a napkin.

The red of ketchup, the eponymous shades of brown sauce, the off-white of tartar.

If Kev was an independent nation, these would be the colours of his flag, a tricolour waving gently in the wake of his wind, a testament to one man's addiction to the sauce.

Sometimes food looks and tastes so bad that you assume it must be incredibly healthy, because nothing pleasant can possibly be good for you, right?

It's similar to when you forced yourself to watch that three-and-a-half-hour long film about an old woman living in occupied Denmark, who very slowly experiences both sorrow *and* regret.

You were so overwhelmingly bored, physically and mentally, by the sustained bout of Scandinavian sadness that you could barely keep your eyes open to read the subtitles.

There is a tendency to assume that by trudging through something difficult and unpleasant you'll somehow be a better person at the end.

Perhaps it's the residual hangover of the Protestant work ethic in effect.

A masochistic impulse lurking within forcing us to believe that our suffering somehow makes us better people or acts as a creative catalyst, eventually turning our pain into great art.

A brief flirtation with quinoa and a never-ending university module on avant-garde cinema taught me long ago that it simply doesn't work that way.

What happens is that you become incapable of escaping the pain.

One of those 'art' people will invite you to a Stan Brakhage retrospective, and even though your body cannot possibly endure it you meekly acquiesce.

Your hand will reach out and put kale into your shopping basket even though it's poison and what you really want is a microwaveable burger and a slice of processed cheese.

It's too late; you're trapped in a state of learned helplessness.

Meet Gareth, a lonely sales rep for a struggling electronics company forever on the road.

He is bursting with desire for Welsh rarebit in the early hours of the morning following some shameful alone time, but adrift in his affordable budget hotel with no room service and no means by which to toast bread and grill mild Cheddar.

Gareth, however, a born improviser, is able to use the heat generated by a company laptop overstimulated by the salesman's niche erotic interests to melt small handfuls of cheese onto his travel-worn white bread.

Gareth had long ago found that the glove compartment of his Rover was just the right size for a loaf of Mighty White.

Along with a few memorised bits of blue humour plucked from the pages of an *FHM* joke book and a family-sized bottle of Brut, it was an essential part of his travelling salesman's kit.

The crispy topping was a combination of dried chilli flakes and a particularly virulent form of scurf, which Gareth had for some time been trying to treat with medicated shampoo.

The faintly cannibalistic crunch was addictive.

It didn't matter that he hadn't sold a single desk fan in more than three weeks, or that it was only a matter of time before he and the few people he called friends lost their jobs.

He had his dandruff-covered cheese on toast; he was complete.

210

If you couldn't already tell by the exotic, ever-so-slightly old-timey packaging on the soft drink can, this sad snapshot comes to us from the USA.

If the tray and its contents look uncomfortably similar to what you might see being served up in the cafeteria on a television show like *Orange Is the New Black*, it's worth bearing in mind that the inmates in those series, and in real life prison, get far more food than the paltry blort of ravioli on display here.

In fact, part of many a prison's plan for dealing with unruly convicts is to stuff them full with a high-calorie diet in the hope that they'll become too bloated and lazy to start stabbing one another or insisting on things like basic human rights.

It's a depressing thought to consider your diet worse than someone who spends the majority of the day wildly oscillating between debilitating boredom and sheer terror at the prospect of getting shanked by the Aryan Brotherhood over an unpaid cockroach-racing debt.

Want to feel worse?

You are in prison.

A prison of the mind, and it's called *consumerism*, yeah?

Yeah.

How's that for an inconvenient truth?

211

Twenty-first century Britain and Hogarth's nightmare of *Gin Lane* is alive and well in a Croydon bedsit.

Gin may now be the hip tipple of choice for the young and terminally twee, but the Georgian era's answer to crack cocaine is still potent stuff.

Sure, it seems like a great laugh to spend the evening in a pop-up bar so exclusive the staff don't even know they're working there, swigging spirits from a jam jar, pretending to ignore Cara Delevingne while surreptitiously photographing her on your phone.

But come the morning, you'll regret having spent the whole night necking test tubes full of Satan's juniper-scented jizz.

The inside of your artfully dishevelled head will be a complete mess and you'll have blown a fat wad of your parents' cash that could have gone on cocaine.

Look, look at what's happened here.

Some trendy young idiot got wrecked at home on Mother's Ruin and ended up burning the toast.

Now they're foolishly attempting to settle their unsteady waters with a frankly ludicrous quantity of soft cheese.

This isn't going to end well.

Soon they'll be pebble-dashing the porcelain, sobbing in pain, cursing the name of Gordon's.

214

Roger felt he enjoyed the finer things in life: 'straight' cigarettes, fresh toenail clippers, and eating dinner barefoot on his highly realistic pine-effect floorboards. He was living life to the full, enjoying his own interpretation of Hunters Chicken, which he felt stripped the dish of all needless pretensions without sacrificing anything in the way of flavour.

Through the years, Roger had lowered his expectations to the point where even an overcooked chicken breast with a meagre spotting of ketchup would feel like a feast fit for a king.

There had been a time some years earlier when Roger had entertained dreams of stardom. He'd attended a few acting classes, got some sexy headshots done, and worked day and night honing the different characters he was to unleash upon an unsuspecting world via a YouTube comedy show.

The videos, however, were not well received, and Roger suffered repeated criticism in the comments section for his rendition of an Irish accent, widely interpreted as sounding Jamaican and condemned by citizens of both countries as 'staggeringly racist'.

Roger's attempts to engage with his critics backfired miserably when he let his temper get the better of him and he berated a journalist from the *Independent*, effectively obliterating his dream of one day landing a comedy-dating show on one of ITV's many subsidiary channels.

Vowing never again to let his hopes get dashed as cruelly as they had, Roger resigned himself to a life of chain-smoking with no socks on.

With greater and greater outrages occurring every day, a deepening divide between rich and poor, and the continued existence of Katie Hopkins, life in Britain was so toxic and deteriorated that most people didn't notice the mushroom clouds looming overhead until it was far too late.

Mark, however, had lived his whole life in Milton Keynes and was therefore well prepared for scraping out a meagre existence in a post-apocalyptic wasteland.

Unlike many of the other survivors he was not so far gone that he had taken to worshipping selfie sticks or using old photographs of Tom Daley as currency.

True, he had to milk a small herd of cats in order to make the cheese (strongly tasting of fish) he smeared onto his cardboard toast; yet it was far preferable to the source he'd seen other more desperate men tap during their quest for sustenance.

Such things haunted Mark.

He paused from his task of foraging for edible roots to watch a two-headed squirrel playing with its Cyclops baby.

Soon he'd return to the well-fortified River Island store that he called home and cook up his cat cheese and onions.

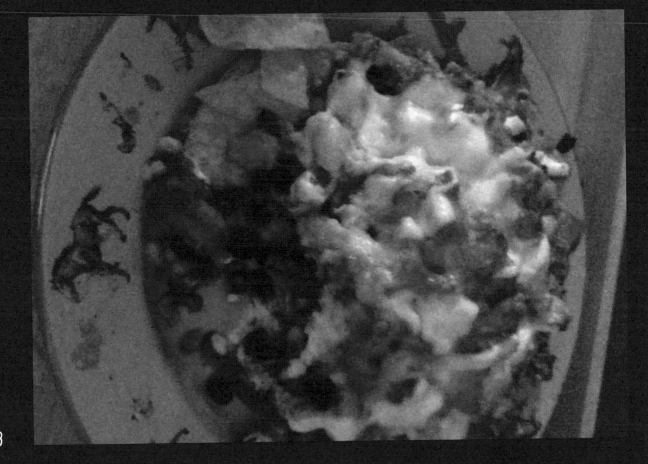

Manuela was not the type of person to do things by halves.

She prided herself on putting 110 per cent effort into everything she did, except when it came to things like understanding how percentages work.

The first to arrive at work, she was always the last to leave too.

Whether or not this was due to the difficulty of being both the sole employee in the finance department of a medium-sized private sixth form college and practically innumerate was beside the point.

It was widely agreed that Manuela's dogged determination had brought her further in life than one would expect of someone who consistently struggled with figuring out how much to tip waiting staff.

The same single-minded focus that had allowed her to overcome what she referred to as 'number blindness' bled into her attitude towards relationships.

Her boyfriend Paul, sick of Manuela's insistence on equine-themed crockery, had tried several times over the years to make a clean break.

At one stage, while the couple were holidaying in Cromer, he went as far as to pull the old abandoned-shoes-on-the-beach ruse in the desperate hope that he could escape her clutches and one day be legally declared dead.

It didn't take, though, and soon he was back to staring at a parade of foals circling a plate of yesterday's nachos, dreaming that a stampede of wild horses might come through the walls of their shared flat and trample him into blissful oblivion.

The packet of powder that came with the cheap noodles from the Chinese supermarket is suspended in the weak broth.

Two hardboiled eggs float aimlessly like a pair of sad eyes in an unloved face.

Tony looks down at his dinner and thinks about getting old.

He thinks about the trappings of his youth that litter his murky bachelor pad.

The American Football helmet from the one term he played at university, encouraged by the American friends he'd made who were only studying overseas for a few short months.

The realisation he was alone playing a sport he couldn't begin to fathom.

The biker jacket hidden away at the back of the wardrobe that had finally succumbed to the flat's rampant mildew.

Tony had never ridden a motorcycle; in fact, reasoning that London had perfectly adequate public transport, he'd never got around to passing his driving test.

Still, he had looked rather fetching riding the bus in black leather and zips.

That was seventeen years and several stones ago.

Putting on the spore-covered coat, Tony finds he now can't zip it up without inhaling to the point of turning purple.

Delicately cleaning off the mould he still can't shift the smell, that lingering stench peculiar to years of neglect and gradual degradation.

Regardless, Tony exudes a strange dignity as he sits eating his eggs and noodles, an awkward plus-sized mannequin dressed like an extra from *The Wild One*.

It's important to treat yourself, to celebrate the small achievements, to break up the monotony of everyday life with a series of little rewards.

We're all ultimately rats in a maze chasing after hunks of dried-out cheese, unaware that at any moment we could be plucked from the comforting banality of routine and have a human ear grafted onto our back.

If we don't look after ourselves every once in a while, who will? Certainly not the people forcing us around the maze, messing with our DNA and making us obese for a laugh.

The carrot we offer ourselves as a means of getting through a miserable life says a lot about us.

Some seek a warm and fuzzy oblivion through alcohol and soft drugs.

Some get their rocks off getting on social media and hurling abuse at minor celebrities and sportspeople who've been publicly shamed for saying something stupid.

Others get that satisfying hit of endorphins from the thrill of bidding on eBay at the last minute for something they don't want simply so that no one else can have it.

This person has much simpler needs. All they need to make a gloomy Sunday feel like a hot Saturday night at Studio 54 is to tip a tin of spaghetti hoops into their bolognese.

If it seems redundant, that's because it is. It adds nothing to the dish save a sickly-sweet lingering aftertaste.

But the simple act of pouring in the hoops and seeing them become one with the wider bolognese? Inexplicably, it makes them feel marginally better about their own chances of getting on in this life.

I'd love to thank the following:
Gav and his horrible-looking food, Bridget Kennedy, Max 'Clingfilm Portent', Guy Trussell,
Richard 'Action' Jackson, the ungrateful Calen Coffman, Anna Marx, Jo Barrow,
Marina O'Loughlin, Chloe Dabbles, Simmy Richman, Lalitha Suhasini, Sonam Savlani, Evan Hunt,
Nils Holmebukt, Mike Didymus, Alexander Alcyone, Ollie Barbieri, Kevin Kenny, Gail Christopher,
Tristan Mortimer, Lara Dickinson, Ruth L. Jones, Mark Sutherland, Matt Williams, Avec Sans,
Gayle Maclean, Christabel Gashion, Tamara Langus and the rest of my family, I suppose,
Stephen Fry, Janis Hopkins, the editors and staff at Tumblr, and everyone who took a picture of
their meal and put it out into the universe only for some stranger to make snide remarks about it.